Speaking of JESUS

How to Tell Your Friends the Best News They Will Ever Hear

J. Mack Stiles

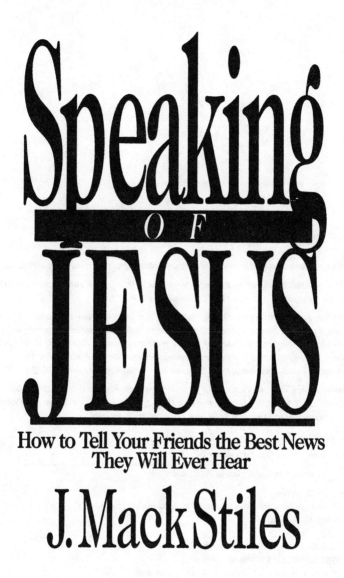

ivp

InterVarsity Press
Downers Grove, Illinois

InterVarsity Press® is the book-publishing division of InterVarsity Christian Fellowship®, a student movement active on campus at hundreds of universities, colleges and schools of nursing in the United States of America, and a member movement of the International Fellowship of Evangelical Students. For information about local and regional activities, write Public Relations Dept., InterVarsity Christian Fellowship, 6400 Schroeder Rd., P.O. Box 7895, Madison, WI 53707-7895.

ISBN 0-8308-1645-3

Printed in the United States of America ∞

Library of Congress Cataloging-in-Publication Data

Stiles, J. Mack, 1956-
    Speaking of Jesus: reaching your world with the good news of
Christ/J. Mack Stiles.
        p.   cm.
    Includes bibliographical references.
    ISBN 0-8308-1645-3 (pbk.: alk. paper)
    1. Witness bearing (Christianity) 2. Evangelistic work.
I. Title.
BV4520.S675   1995
269'.2—dc20   95-16640
                                                                                        CIP

20	19	18	17	16	15	14	13	12	11	10	9	8	7	6	5	4	3
11	10	09	08	07	06	05	04	03	02	01	00	99	98	97	96		

To Leeann,
whose strength has carried me.

Acknowledgments

This book has been a family event. Leeann's care and love, Mom's Dad's and my two sisters' undying belief in me, Leeann's parents' constant encouragement, and the sweet prayers of my young sons, Tristan, David and Isaac, have all helped thoughts become a book.

The family of First Alliance Church, Lexington, has spurred me on too. Pastor Ron Gifford generously allowed me the use of his pulpit so I could express new ideas. The Koinonia class gave me enthusiastic feedback. Our small group—the Bunges, Garners, Hannas, Spelers and Tsangs—prayed me through this book from beginning to end.

This book is a product of years with the family of InterVarsity. The Tennessee and Kentucky I-V teams have been the crucible for me as I've figured out evangelism. Staffworkers invested their lives in me when I was a student. And when I became a staffworker with I-V, my supervisors and pastors helped me grow. Glen Spidell, Dave Moore and Ken Schmitt stand out in my mind. Paul Tokunaga helped me from the very first steps. Then there was the help of two former staffworkers turned editors, Andy Le Peau and Linda Doll. Their insight and graciousness touched this book and my heart.

Two staff couples have contributed to this book in important ways: David and Angie McNeill and Brian and Joanne Parks, people who have been colaborers in the ministry of the gospel in Tennessee, Kentucky and overseas. Of all friends they know me the best—and still love me. They have listened, corrected, encouraged. For their friendship and tutelage I am grateful.

Then there is the family of supporters. Their gifts, love and prayers have made it possible for me to be a staffworker. Two people in particular have taken time to be a part of our ministry with I-V: Ted and Judi Callahan. From the campus to the Urbana missions conference to the sands of North Africa, their support has been invaluable.

Many others from the I-V family who helped shape this book are mentioned in the following pages. I was especially touched by the help of the Marshall family as we remembered Judee together.

The real reason this book came about was university students. The world of the university is the anvil where I am hammering out my thoughts about evangelism. Students are great teachers. I'm grateful for the opportunity to call their home my mission field.

• Part I •

Engaging
Our
Worlds

At one time we too were foolish, disobedient, deceived
and enslaved by all kinds of passions and
pleasures. We lived in malice and envy, being hated
and hating one another. But when the kindness and love
of God our Savior appeared, he saved us,
not because of righteous things we had done, but
because of his mercy. He saved us through
the washing of rebirth and renewal by the Holy Spirit,
whom he poured out on us generously through
Jesus Christ our Savior, so that, having been justified by
his grace, we might become heirs having
the hope of eternal life. This is a trustworthy saying.
And I want you to stress these things, so that those who
have trusted in God may be careful to devote
themselves to doing what is good. These things are excellent and profitable for everyone. (Tit 3:3-8)

• One •

Blowing Smoke

Twenty years ago I thought that sharing my faith was in bad taste. "My religion is a personal thing," I heard people say. And I agreed. I never stopped to think about all the other personal things I talked freely about: fears, family, girlfriends. My religion *is* a personal thing, deeply personal, but it's not private. I've learned a lot in twenty years.

I was skiing in Aspen, Colorado. I was seventeen years old. After a good day on the slopes my ski buddy, Henry, and I hiked down the concrete stairwell of the condominium. Our destination was the basement arcade and teen hangout.

Between the third and fourth floors we met a ski bum smoking a joint. He rasped, in that funny voice you get when you try to talk and hold in the smoke, "Man, I'm glad you guys showed up. This is fine weed. I couldn't have done it myself." Out of courtesy we helped him finish smoking it. Elevated, the three of us continued our descent to the arcade room.

Henry and I banged away at a game of Foosball, but the little plastic soccer players didn't hold our attention for long. We migrated to the group of people by the pool table—a group of teens talking.

Some of the discussion was about skiing. How cold it was on the chair lift. What kind of spill someone had taken on Ruthie's Run. The look of a compound fracture (to impress the women present). Soon the conversation took a more philosophical turn. Henry, never at a loss for opinions, began offering his.

At some point someone started talking about religion. I might have ignored the comments except Henry pointed his finger at me and exclaimed, "If you want to talk about religion, you need to talk to Mack. He's a Christian." My heart sank.

A few months before this confrontation in the condo basement, I had had another talk with a guy my age. His name was Robert. Robert explained to me that Christianity went beyond a system of do's and don'ts. He told me the heart of Christianity was a relationship with Jesus. This was news to me. Rules left me cold, but a friendship with God—that was just what I was looking for. I prayed with Robert that August night. Though the exact words of my prayer now escape me, I remember telling Jesus I wanted to follow him. It was the beginning of our journey together.

My prayer was real. The relationship began, but knowing Jesus didn't give me an infusion of theology. Basic Christian concepts were as distant as the moon. I was at a loss to find John 3:16 in the Bible. Lordship sounded like the name of a boat. St. Paul was a church somewhere. I had talked a bit with Henry about my experience, yet defending *my* faith, much less *the* Faith, seemed best left to religious professionals.

But it was too late. The teens in the arcade room fixed their attention on me. The red eyes of our ski bum friend went wide. The others raised their eyebrows. The battle lines were drawn: Mack, defender of the faith, against the unbelieving pagans of Aspen, Colorado. *Oh well,* I thought, *I owe God a favor.*

The conversation went like this:

Aspenite #1:	Christianity is stupid.
Mack:	Is not.
Aspenite #1:	It's stupid to believe in something you can't see.
Mack:	(stumped look)
Aspenite #2:	I don't go to church because all the people there are hypocrites.
Mack:	Are not.
Aspenite #2:	Are too.

I was losing ground. I needed to go on the offensive.

Mack:	Maybe they are where you come from, but not the Christians I know.
Crowd:	(hoots of) Yeah, they are. (and) Gimme a break, man.
Mack:	(pointing finger at group) I'll tell you who's not a hypocrite . . . Christians filled with the Holy Ghost!

Delivery of this last sentence came with such religious dignity and lowering of voice the others began to look uneasy. They didn't respond. How could they? They didn't know what I was talking about. It was a good thing. I didn't know what I was talking about either. It even appeared I had put them in their place.

Mack:	(with a victorious smirk) Come on, Henry, let's go find something to eat. I got the munchies.

So ended my first try at evangelism.

The word *witness* is a legal term. It means someone who has had firsthand experience—often an eyewitness. When you say a Christian is a witness, you mean that he or she has experienced something directly. In the arcade I talked about things I had not witnessed. And I didn't talk about things I *had* witnessed.

Another mistake was living my life differently from what I proclaimed. The biggest hypocrite was not in church but in Aspen. Is it any wonder, with an example like mine, that Henry rejected my later attempts to tell him about Christ? Henry went on to college and then to Harvard to get his MBA. He now works with Hollywood actors and producers—people whose films have influenced society. Would the world be a different place if my witness had been more consistent?

Sharing our faith is not about winning battles. God is very capable of defending himself. Our job is to win hearts, not act as God's defense attorney. I did more damage in that one skirmish than I knew.

Another Attempt

Twenty years later, my wife, Leeann, and I were serving dinner to friends. The phone rang.

"Hello, Mack. It's Linda." I heard highway noises mixed with the sound of my sister's strained voice. I can always tell when she calls from her car phone.

"Are you busy?" she asked.

"No, not really," I lied. "What's up?"

"Well, I was wondering if I could, umm, pop over?"

Linda is a successful accountant. She works with a CPA firm. Order and discipline mark Linda. Popping over is not her style. For all I could remember, this was the first time in her life that she had asked to pop anywhere. Something was wrong.

"Sure, we'd love to see you. Is anything the matter?" I asked.

"Well, I just had a bad day at work. I haven't been home. I don't even feel like going home. I had a tiff, well, an argument, really, with the other partner and I . . . I just need to get out of town."

We used the time with our friends to pray for my sister. I didn't say much new. I had been praying for Linda almost two decades.

An hour or so later I opened the door to greet her. Linda was standing on the front porch finishing her cigarette. Her Mazda RX7 convertible glistened under the streetlight behind her. She looked edgy.

"Come on in. Our guests are about to leave, and Leeann wants to get the kids ready for bed," I said.

Linda spent some time with her three nephews while Leeann and I said goodby to our friends. Then, when Linda and I were alone, I started probing. "Tell me what's going on."

She sighed and then said, "I don't know . . . bad day at work, I guess."

"Is that all?"

She started softly, "No, not really. I feel so confused. I feel all jumbled up inside." She sighed and looked out the window. "After the divorce I decided I was going to make some changes in my life. I'm really trying, but it . . . doesn't seem to be working."

Linda stopped twisting the absent ring on her finger and folded her hands.

"I've started going to church. I even like it . . . sometimes. I just don't understand a lot of . . ." Her voice trailed off. She looked out the window. She was blinking back tears now.

"What else?" I asked.

"Oh, I don't know." Now as she talked she opened and closed her hands. "I'm trying to read my Bible." She gave a sad laugh and rolled her eyes. "It's like reading the phone book."

I smiled. "What else?"

Then it happened.

"Oh!" she almost shouted. It was the sound of someone wounded, of someone who is carrying agonizing news. "Oh," she said again, now crying, "I'm just so ashamed of my life." She looked up at the ceiling and then buried her face in her hands. "I'm just *so ashamed of my life,*" she whispered.

The pain in her sobs was piercing. Tears were in my eyes now too.

I managed to choke out, "Linda, please, let me tell you about the One who came to take away our shame."

"I'm ready. I really am. I guess that's why I'm here," she said. "I've watched you guys. At first I thought it was some kind of show, but you guys are different."

"Linda, the place to start a new life is with Jesus. It's very hard to make sense of the Bible, or of church, or even of our own lives if we don't know Jesus. Has there ever been a point when you turned your life over to Jesus and gave him permission to run it?"

She said, "No, I don't think so. I do believe that he's God. But I don't think I've ever given him my life."

"That's the place to start, then," I said.

"Okay, I'm really ready." She clenched both hands now.

"There are some things I want you to understand before you do. Is that all right?" I asked. She nodded.

Linda and I went through a simple summary of the gospel: God, People, Christ, Response and Cost. It really could have been any kind of outline, because it was not technique or fancy words that propelled Linda but the Spirit of God.

Then I said, "Let's talk to God together. You can do that silently, or I can pray a prayer that you can repeat, or you can say your own prayer."

Linda said, "I think I need to say it aloud. But I don't know if I have the words. If you pray aloud I'll . . . I'll make the prayer mine."

Our prayer was kin to my own first prayer years before. Linda did make our prayer her own.

"Lord, we have made a mess of life," I started.

"Lord, I have made a mess of my life," she repeated.

"Lord, we are grateful for your death on the cross," I said.

"Lord," Linda was now saying each word forcefully, "I'm so grateful for your death on the cross."

To the sounds of my sons splashing in the tub upstairs—and angel choruses higher still—Linda stated a simple prayer of rebirth. Elapsed time: maybe fifteen minutes. Effect on time: all eternity.

When Linda looked up, tears were hanging on the end of her nose. She said, "Man, that was intense. I need a cigarette!" Then she gave me a flustered look (me being the religious one in the family). "That's not right, is it?" she asked.

"Well, let me say that you might start looking to Jesus, not me, for answers to questions like that. I do have a recommendation, though," I answered.

"Tell me."

"You've got a lot of things to work on in your life. I would suggest that you pick just one area to start with and give it to Jesus. I have a hunch that it might be bigger than smoking."

Motivated by her nicotine fit, Linda nodded her agreement and smoked another cigarette on the front porch. It was her first act as a new Christian.

Some First Steps

Linda, Leeann and I started meeting weekly for Bible study and prayer. Linda found a good church. After reading John White's book *The Fight,* she decided to give the Lord her time. She told Jesus that she would meet with him each day. Her relationship with God grew.

It wasn't long before Linda realized that God was tapping her shoulder and demanding the cigarettes. She had smoked for her entire adult life. She had tried to quit once. It lasted a day. Now she felt afraid that the Lord wasn't powerful enough to overcome her smoking, but she decided to set a date, recruit people to pray, and quit. That's exactly what she did. Later she commented, "Mack, it was almost too easy. You can't believe the power of the Lord if you haven't known it before." I believe it. I have seen God's power at work in the life of my sister.

As I contrast my evangelistic attempts with Henry and with Linda, I see I've learned a lot. I find I can trust God's timing in people's lives—for years if need be—because the Spirit, not Mack, is the propelling power in rebirth.

I've discovered I don't need to answer all questions. In fact, it's probably best to ask some. I shudder to think how easy it would have been to give Linda a book like *Church Shopping Made Easy* or a brief overview on how to understand the Scriptures. But I wanted to introduce my sister to Jesus, not biblical hermeneutics.

Some might say I led my sister to Christ and then encouraged her to go smoke, but I've learned to trust God's work in the hearts of those open to him.

Foundations and Models

I'm grateful for the Lord's patient hand in my own wandering and slow steps. I'm grateful for the Lord's forgiveness of my outright sin too. The only way I could tell Linda about the One who came to take away our shame is to know personal shame myself and to have him take it away. In part one of this book we'll look at these foundations for sharing our faith.

I didn't know much theology as a new Christian, but I've come to recognize its importance. I've found John 3:16. I'm captivated by the way Jesus revealed himself. I think his conversation in the following chapter, John 4, provides an exceptional look at the attitudes of Jesus toward sharing our faith. We'll study his words from that chapter in part two.

I met the man called Paul in the Scriptures and pondered his love and fire. I found some good reasons for naming churches after him. Paul saw the Christian as an ambassador. He knew our words and lives represent Christ. We'll look at Paul's model for sharing our faith in part three.

I have learned a lot in twenty years. After all, mistakes are wonderful teachers. I hope that my mistakes can be your teachers. I want to save you a decade or two. Not that I'm there yet—there's a lot more to learn. More mistakes are in the making, but I'm working toward my goal: to speak of Jesus in a way people can hear.

Questions for Reflection or Discussion

1. What contrasts do you notice between Mack's evangelistic efforts in Aspen and with his sister twenty years later?
2. What do you think was Mack's biggest area of growth?
3. In what ways would you like to grow in your own outreach efforts?

Pray that God will help you grow in the area of evangelism.

• Two •

First Steps

The first step of evangelism was not to start blabbing—my ski slope disaster showed me that. It was to come to grips with Christ's claim on my life. Lordship, it was called, and I discovered the lordship of Jesus was a far more powerful tool for evangelism than any arguments in his defense.

After my failed evangelistic effort in Aspen, I decided to get my spiritual act together. I joined an active church youth group. They seemed a strange and holy crew to me—full of exotic religious jargon and out-loud prayers—but they loved me and helped me grow. We struggled together to make sense of new faith in real life.

It intrigued me to discover they endorsed evangelism—that is, until I found out they also endorsed tracts with cartoons. I found these tracts unsatisfying and trivial at best; at worst they offended. "So, this is evangelism?" I wondered.

I needed to get a Bible, so I ferreted out the local Christian bookstore. I was standing at the Bible rack deciding which Bible to buy when I spied the rack on evangelism. Since my newfound youth group emphasized the need to share our faith, I surveyed the books.

Wincing at titles like *The Soul Winner,*[1] I began my beeline for the door. But as I turned to go, a title grabbed me: *How to Give Away Your Faith.* That title was not a collaring of unwilling souls, but a generous offer. I bought it (along with the biggest Bible on the rack, complete with maps, cross-references and enigmatic charts on the Second Coming).

Getting Things in Order

To my surprise, the author said evangelism is a call for all believers, not an optional accessory to the Christian life. Paul Little talked about commitment to Christ *before* we share our faith. He said to be effective in evangelism we need to be sold out to Christ.

I also began reading the big Bible I bought. God and Little seemed to agree.

"But in your hearts set apart Christ as Lord. Always be prepared to give an answer to everyone who asks you to give the reason for the hope that you have. But do this with gentleness and respect" (1 Pet 3:15).

Well, it couldn't get much clearer than that. This verse linked the idea of lordship with evangelism. That is, we set Christ as the Lord (or leader) of our lives and prepare to speak about him with reason, respect and gentleness.

Before I even finished the book, I bowed my head, confessed to God my arrogance and said I would follow him as Lord of my life—even in evangelism. God didn't waste time answering that prayer.

At that same moment God was pursuing someone else: John, the older brother of my ski buddy, Henry.

John the Atheist

I had admired John during high school. He was a member of a rock-and-roll band. He was a snow skier. John carried a card saying he was an atheist and a chip on his shoulder saying his position came more from rebellion than from intellect.

Our culture believes, incorrectly, that doubt is more honest than faith. Perhaps that's why atheists seem smarter than everyone else. At any rate, others in high school considered John an intellectual.

John and I took an advanced English class together one year. "Advanced" meant shoot the bull, since that's mostly what we did.

Religion was a regular subject of our readings, so it became a regular debate in class. It took the reading of *Siddhartha* by Hermann Hesse for the class to square off. Atheists sat on one side of the room, and Tom, a guy from my youth group, sat on the other. I cowered in the muddled middle.

During the hot debate one student, Alan, announced, "I'll give God three minutes to show up; otherwise, I refuse to believe in him." Alan dramatically held up his arm and stared at his watch.

I'm glad God didn't show up the way Alan wanted him to, for "who can stand in the presence of the Lord?" (1 Sam 6:20). But God *was* present, and Tom knew it. With wisdom beyond his years, Tom said, "Alan, God has shown up; he's talking to you through me. That's his way, you know—he uses people." I don't remember Alan's response, but I do remember John's smirk.

John surprised no one when he decided to attend Rhodes College, a heady liberal arts school in Memphis, Tennessee. After his first year, John visited me and encouraged me to attend

Rhodes too. Now that *was* surprising.

I was planning to attend the University of Colorado. Visions of ski slopes danced in my head. But with John's encouragement I decided it couldn't hurt to apply to Rhodes. I doubted if I could get in, so it was easy to tell God I would go if accepted. Gold-medal dreams gave way to God's plans in flat Memphis when my acceptance letter arrived.

John's first year at Rhodes had proved tough on his atheistic faith. Not because Rhodes is a particularly Christian place. In fact, some professors shredded Christians in class with textual criticism of Scripture. John's atheism faced a different challenge. His first class was an extended Western Civ course. Part of the course curriculum involved reading the Bible—dangerous stuff for an atheist. The evidence of Scripture triggered John's doubts about his atheism. But what really challenged him was the growing sense that God was after him. John would later refer to poet Francis Thompson's concept of God as "the hound of heaven."

Unlikely Encounter

John hitchhiked on weekends to see his girlfriend in Kentucky. Sometimes rides were few. One slow day in September John accepted a ride from a Jesus freak.

Jesus freaks were a particular phenomenon of the seventies. Many aspects of Jesus-freak subculture reflected the times. They had the same countercultural air and shoulder-length hair as the radicals of the time. They suspended big wooden crosses from loops of leather around their necks. Their eyes had the same free, wild look—not from a drug-induced high but from the excitement of their relationship with Christ.

This Jesus freak was no different. He knew deliverance. Jesus was his Lord. He told John, "I want you to know that Jesus has healed me of heroin addiction." This man's arms bore the scars from his heroin injections. His face bore joy from the freedom Christ granted. His car bore an uncomfortable atheist who was a captive audience for a long ride.

Today John can barely remember what the Jesus freak looked like. What stands out in John's mind is the vibrancy of his faith.

John remained uncomfortable for the entire weekend. He felt the hound of heaven in full pursuit, but he greased the uneasy feelings with weekend sex and then returned to school.

Weeks later those suspicious thoughts of God's pursuit mushroomed to full terror. John was hitchhiking again on highway 52. Finally, a car pulled over with two guys in the front seat. John tossed his backpack through the open door and jumped in.

To his shock, there in the driver's seat sat the same Jesus freak. Some "coincidences" are too much even for atheists. The Jesus freak slung his arm over the front seat, grinned at John and stated the obvious: "God's after you, man."

As they drove down the road, the other passenger, an African-American, told John he had been in a local jail. The Jesus freak—whom he didn't know—had just showed up at jail and bailed him out. Now the Jesus freak was giving him a lift home.

Turning to John, he said, "White folk don't do that for black folk, you know." And then, "I don't know what he's got, but I want it."

John went claustrophobic. "Let me out of the car."

The Jesus freak said, "You're in the middle of nothing but cornfields, man; you ain't going nowhere."

This was the truth physically and spiritually, and it rocked John. "No," he protested, "this is where I get out."

The Hound of Heaven Gives Chase

John stood dumbly at the roadside until the car was out of sight over the next hill. He then shucked his backpack and ran wildly through the stalks of corn. After some time he fell to his knees, exhausted. Looking up, he searched the sky. "Who are you?" he shouted. And then in a frightened whisper, "What do you want with me?"

Maybe John didn't notice, but his waning atheism was dead. He was praying. And his prayer, though angry, was honest and soon to be answered.

I suppose I was the answer. My youth-group friend Tom was right, back in high-school English: God uses people, with all their faults, to reveal the good news.

When we met at Rhodes, John wanted to talk about God. I should have wondered why this atheist had so suddenly changed his tune. Was it the tremendous evangelistic technique I had developed? No, I was just available.

A walk around the campus one late afternoon and evening with John is a vivid memory. Rhodes sits across from the Memphis Zoo. At times in the late evenings you could hear noises from monkeys, peacocks, an occasional large cat. Maybe that's why the memory has such a wild feel. Maybe it's just because the Spirit was working.

"John," I said, "if you really want to follow God, you gotta stop getting high and sleeping with your girlfriend."

"Why?" said John.

"Well, you can't do that stuff and follow Jesus."

"Okay," he said.

I said, "You need to give your life to Jesus. It's not good enough just to agree that he exists. You need to pray; give him your whole life."

"Okay, I will," said John.

And he did . . .

In fact, I have an old Bible John gave me while we were students at Rhodes. It contains this inscription:

To my brother and friend Mack Stiles, who brought the word which changed my life to accept the counsel of God. For his 19th birthday. John.

What made the difference for John? My great evangelistic technique? No, I was still working it out. I had made a commitment to Christ as my Lord. So I was available to share with John what I understood, and God used it. But the main human instrument in John's turning to Christ was not me at all, but an unknown Jesus freak on highway 52.

That young believer's love of Christ is the same place all of us start. The most effective action in evangelism is having a deep and vibrant faith. So we start with lordship—not a gospel outline or an evangelistic method, but Christ. *Our first step of evangelism is to yield to Christ's lordship.*

Lordship is just another way to say the first commandment, "Love the LORD your God with all your heart and with all your soul and with all your strength" (Deut 6:5). We cultivate this commitment to Christ's lordship in our life in some important ways.

Jesus said that if we love him we'll do what he says. This can take some very strange turns. Following God is a strange business, filled with wonder. I often see myself in the disciples as they puzzle over the direction Jesus takes, be it avoiding popularity at Capernaum or marching madly to a cross in Jerusalem. His ways don't always make sense to us, but that's okay—there are more important things than what makes sense. His ways are not our ways, that's for sure—but his ways are always better.

Today, when John and I reminisce about our campus walk, John says the most important thing I told him was, "John, you gotta stop . . ." In essence I said, "John, if you want to follow God you must agree to go his way."

Here are four steps to take as you follow Jesus (we'll talk more about them in chapter seventeen):

1. Practice spiritual disciplines. The practice of spiritual disciplines is a key to our spiritual vitality. Among other things, spiritual disciplines include prayer, Bible reading, meditation, giving, silence and solitude, fasting and confession. These are things of spiritual health practiced by our Lord and required of those who would follow him. Reading that big Bible was one of the most important things I did. It still is.

2. Give yourself to a community of believers. I don't mean *just* join a church. I mean give your life for other believers. That youth group I joined was flawed. If it had been perfect it would have become flawed the moment I joined. But they were the body of Christ, and they loved me and I loved them. That's far more important than whether they used tracts with or without cartoons. Jesus prayed for us, "That all of them may be one, Father, just as you are in me and I am in you. May they also be in us so that the world may believe that you have sent me" (Jn 17:21). Our greatest witness to the world is Christian community.

3. Share your faith. We have a part to play in God's rescue plan. As Paul Little says, "Evangelism is one of the keys to spiritual health."[2] The foundation of our job description in evangelism is the topic of the next chapter.

4. Dare to take a risk. To each of these areas I would add risk. Never stop risking for God. Jesus is risky. When we take him as Lord, he calls us to lay down our lives—for our own sake. Jesus said, "For what will it profit them if they gain the whole world but forfeit their life? Or what will they give in return for their life?" (Mt 16:26 NRSV). A sure-fire way to keep your faith vibrant is to risk your life. Risk your time, your place, your pride, your money. Risk sharing the good news with others. Don't stop. For one thing, you never get "there." You'll never stop growing with

Christ. He's just too big. Risking our lives on Christ's lordship is what faith is all about: it keeps us vibrant.

John and I, today, wonder what happened to that Jesus freak. How did he feel after he left John on the side of the road? Did he feel guilty for offending a non-Christian? Perhaps he felt ashamed that he lost an opportunity to tell John all the facts of the gospel. Though it was clear God was after John, did he wonder if he had blown it? Did he wish he had spent more time brushing up on his technique? Maybe he did.

If he were here today, I would tell him this: "More important than the language you used was your vibrant love for God. More important than how much of the gospel you had a chance to articulate were your actions of love. More important than all the techniques in the world was your clear commitment to Christ as Lord."

Questions for Reflection or Discussion
1. Name some links in God's chain that brought John to Christ.
2. What links went together in God's chain to bring you to Christ?
3. The lordship of Christ was a major link in John's conversion. How did's Mack's commitment to lordship and the Jesus freak's commitment to lordship fit together?

How might your commitment to lordship become a link in the chain for someone else? Pray that this will happen.

• Three •

A Father's
Rescue

After we are committed to Christ as Lord, we need to understand our personal barriers to evangelism and some ways to pull those barriers down. I'd like to approach this problem with a true-to-life parable.

I grew up in a small western Kentucky city on the Ohio River. The distance from the Kentucky shore to the Indiana shore was about a mile. The river's movement was massive but quiet. Sometimes it looked as if the land was flowing by, not the river. It was an illusion, of course. Water and floating river rubbish slipped by with surprising speed.

A mile downstream from our town, the water funneled through a sluiceway in a dam. There the river became a deadly passage. I remember watching waterlogged trees thrown into the air as the entire muddy Ohio River cascaded over this rude interruption in its journey. Sometimes the *Messenger & Inquirer* would report that some hapless boater or fisherman had drowned going over the dam.

The river was safe enough for those who were cautious. During the summer it was our playground. We treated it more like a lake. We spent our time upstream, away from the dam. Our family had two boats: a sailboat my father had built by hand and a multipurpose runabout. Dad would say our runabout was good for everything and perfect for nothing. We spent weekends exploring islands and sandbars. We sailed when the wind was right and motored when it wasn't.

Every spring Dad would haul both boats out of storage and put them into the water for their annual tune-up. Dad and I were a team. He would maneuver the car so motorboat and trailer went into the water. I would gun the outboard engine, floating the boat free.

One blustery spring day Dad backed the boat into the river. The old two-cycle engine sputtered and came alive for the first time that year. I slid the boat off the trailer into the Ohio. Turning the boat around, I imprudently made an arc out into the river before steering back to the dock. Midway the engine died.

It was then that I noticed the river's swiftness. The spring floods filled it with power. The current caught the powerless boat and swirled it in circles. At the same time, a stiff wind pushed the boat downstream. I grabbed the key and cranked the engine. The battery, weak from its winter hibernation, quickly lost its power. Then I heard the roar from the dam.

Dad was running along the bank of the river, trying to keep up with the boat. Though I wasn't close enough to see his face, his movements betrayed his fear. My father is the kind of person you want to be with in an emergency, cool-headed and quick-witted. So seeing *him* frightened escalated my fear. Hands cupped around his mouth, he was yelling instructions to me while stumbling over roots and rocks. But the words swirled away with the wind.

I took off the engine cover. "Maybe I can start it by hand," I thought. I didn't have enough strength.

The river was moving faster now. The warning buoys bobbed by. The peril of the dam was written on the buoys in capital letters: DANGER! DO NOT GO PAST THIS POINT. I panicked. Unable to find a paddle, I grabbed a water ski and flayed the water. But my efforts were hopeless against the power of the river.

After what seemed like hours, I heard a thumping noise against the boat, but it didn't register. The sound of one boat bumping another was one I knew well, but now, in my hysteria, I continued my moronic paddling—until Dad's head appeared above the bow. He looped a line around the cleat, smiled a reassuring smile and began towing our crippled craft back to the dock. Dad had pirated a small, smelly fishing boat from the dockhouse.

Though the trip back to the dock took some time, I was still trembling when we arrived.

I said, "I got scared."

He said, "Everything's okay."

I noticed his voice was hoarse. He'd lost it yelling, *"Throw out the anchor!"*

I felt pretty silly about forgetting the anchor, but sometimes that's the way life is. Sometimes we need a rescue, not instructions, and Dad had rescued me. I was saved by my father.

The flow of biblical history tells a story of a loving Father rescuing his lost children from disaster. The rescue began in Genesis when the tempter was told his head would be crushed by a child of Eve. The law of Moses pointed to our need for a rescue. The prophets warned of disaster and pointed to one who would rescue—but they were just shouting from the shore. The rescue took place with the arrival of Jesus. Jesus, at the direction of his Father, offered his life as a ransom for the world and rescued God's people. Stop and think. When you share your faith you are taking part in the heart and history of God; you are taking part in a divine rescue. And God will go to fantastic lengths—even putting himself in danger—to see his loved ones back safe with him.

Wrong Views of Evangelism

Most people today have a negative view of evangelists and evangelism. I used to rank among them. I remember the first time I noticed the word as a new believer. It was in my big King James Bible. I saw the book of John, titled *The Gospel According to Saint John the Evangelist,* and thought to myself, *Funny, I thought John was the nice one, you know, the one Jesus loved.*

The word *evangelist* has come to mean a type of Christian profession: missionaries, pastors, evangelists. Their job is to see large numbers of people converted. Names such as George Whitefield, D. L. Moody and Billy Graham come to mind.

Who wouldn't feel intimidation if we all had to be Billy Graham? The guy is fantastic, a once-a-century paragon of virtue and success. Thank the Lord for Billy Graham. Thank the Lord the Lord doesn't want the rest of us to be Billy! The Lord wants us to be faithful—in our own way, in our own world.

In addition, it seemed I'd need a seminary degree before God could use me to share my faith. Didn't I need answers to questions about the Spanish Inquisition, the doctrine of propitiation and the psychological dynamics of conversion? This overwhelmed me.

These negative or inflated views of evangelism and evangelists hindered me from taking part in God's rescue. They justified my thought "Evangelism just isn't my gift." (It was like saying, "Helping people in trouble just isn't my gift.")

Perhaps you feel the same. Loaded with guilt, sensing that really there is some better way to share your faith but not knowing how, you throw up your hands in despair and leave it to the professionals.

But this is not God's view of evangelism, nor is it his desire. Evangelism is not reserved only for the learned, the famous or the powerful. God desires ordinary heroes in his rescue operation. Part of our problem in evangelism is a confusion in job descriptions—ours with the Holy Spirit's.

Get Your Job Description Right

When I first made a commitment to evangelism, equipped with my gift for gab and motivated by a guilty conscience, I launched into various evangelistic schemes.

"Mack witnesses to lampposts if people aren't around," one friend gushed. At that point I viewed evangelism as a function of right technique and results. I saw the burden of salvation resting solely on me. It just seemed I should present the gospel in a way to get people to convert. If no one converted, evangelism had not taken place. But I sensed something was missing. *Is this evangelism?* I wondered.

On a dare from a fellow student, I signed up as a counselor for a Billy Graham movie. Our role was to go forward when the call was made at the end of the movie and explain to folk how to receive Christ. To be counselors, though, we first received training.

Our trainer was Brother Grey (for months I thought that "Brother" was his first name). Brother Grey commented offhandedly, "We must remember *it's the Holy Spirit working in the hearts of people to produce salvation, not us.*"The missing piece clicked into place and set off an explosion in my head. No wonder I felt so guilty and driven . . . I had adopted the Holy Spirit's job description!

J. I. Packer says it like this:

Our evangelistic work is the instrument that He uses for this purpose [of salvation], but the power that saves is not in the instrument: it is in the hand of the One who uses the instrument. We must not at any stage forget that. For if we forget that it is God's prerogative to give results when the gospel is preached, we shall start to think that it is our responsibility to secure them. . . . [And] our approach to evangelism would become pragmatic and calculating.[1]

The Holy Spirit starts, develops and gives birth to salvation. The Holy Spirit, not me. This simple bit of good theology helped me begin shedding my compulsion to convict people of their sin, drag them to Christ and force them to cry out from their hearts in faith (a truly impossible job description for a human).

Unlike the Holy Spirit's job description, ours is relatively simple. First we follow Christ as Lord; *then* we proclaim the truth of Christ. It's our hope that hearers will turn to God in faith, but their response is not our responsibility.

I didn't need a technique to manipulate others with crafty questions. I was free to be myself and to share the story of Christ in my own words, from my own experience. You can imagine my great relief to know that God, not I, was working his plans in people.

But that leaves us with the question "What is our job description?" Let's think about my river rescue as an extended parable of evangelism.

Available

Dad knew all I needed to do to stop a disaster was throw out an anchor. If he had shouted more loudly would I have been rescued? No, I couldn't hear, so shouting wise instructions from the shore didn't help. It took crossing some barriers and a willingness to put himself in danger to come get me.

God asks the same of us in evangelism. God wants us available to people, not shouting instructions at them. (They often can't understand what we're talking about at first, anyway.) He wants us to *get into others' lives*. He may not ask us to steal a boat, but he may ask us to cross some conventional boundaries. If we are willing to risk our comfort to get into other people's worlds with the truth we bear, we'll be a more powerful witness than all the instruction manuals in the world.

Equipped

Was a luxury yacht needed to rescue me on the river? The well-used fishing boat was available. It worked fine.

My father, untrained in river rescue and without a choice of fancy boats, did what was needed. He used his wits and common sense. He used the tools at hand.

That's what God is asking of us. He *does* want us equipped to share the message of his rescue. But he wants us to use what we have. You may not be a trained professional in the business of sharing your faith. But if you share what you know about your relationship with Christ, when the opportunity comes, God will use you—seminary degree not required.

Motivated

Would others watching from the shore have responded the way Dad did? No, not likely: "It's not our job. We're not trained. We don't have the right equipment. It's just not our gift."

But that described my dad too. The other people watching me from the shore couldn't feel what my father did. He was motivated by his love for his child to overcome the barriers and dangers that would have made someone else say, "It's too risky." That made the difference: Dad rescued me because he loved me and wanted me safe.

That's what God wants for us. God wants us motivated in the right way: not by guilt trips or with gritting-of-teeth or a whipped-up frenzy, but by love. The same kind of love my dad felt yelling from the bank.

Ordinary Heroes

Dad was an ordinary hero. He was available to me in spite of danger; he used the tools at his disposal; and he was motivated by his love.

When God calls us to share our faith, he doesn't care about our credentials or how our fancy our programs look. He doesn't care how loud we can shout. He doesn't even care if it's not our gift. He just wants us to recognize those in need around us and respond with what we have.

Over the years I've seen many folks struggle to share their faith. Some were experts in one area only to fail miserably in another. For instance, some were great apologists for the faith but didn't know any non-Christians. Others were in contact with non-Christians but didn't seem to know what to say about spiritual issues. Others just didn't care.

But there were some who seemed to have put all three parts together. They knew the message of Christ and could defend it. They were comfortable with non-Christians. They were motivated by the love of Christ for the people they knew.

These are the ordinary heroes of evangelism. I call these people "engagers." They were the ones who seemed to be leading people to Christ—not the masses, understand, but individuals along life's way. Others pegged them as having the gift of evangelism, but when you talked to these engagers they usually said, "No, I'm just obedient." I've learned a lot from them.

I'm convinced that the gift of evangelism is not needed in order for a person to be a faithful witness of Christ. These three areas (availability to non-Christians, prepared and equipped minds, and right motivation) are the critical mix for evangelism and the foundational framework for my understanding for evangelism. Our job description for real-life evangelism is to be equipped, available and motivated.

Diagnosing Your Evangelistic Condition

Each of these three categories in evangelism is important. Without one of the three, evangelistic efforts can be as unstable as a three-legged stool missing a leg.

I've put these three categories together as an evangelism diagnostic tool. Here's how to use it.

Step One: Ask yourself about your strengths and weaknesses in the following areas when it comes to sharing your faith. Circle + as strong and - as weak:

☐ Motivated (I have a heartfelt desire to share the good news of Christ): + or -

☐ Available (I have social contact with non-Christians): + or -

☐ Equipped (I can effectively explain the message): + or -

Step Two: Take your three answers and find your "diagnosis" on chart 1 (p. 40). The chart gives these three categories some shape. Negatives in one or more areas cripple our efforts to share our faith. The chart demonstrates how our strengths and weaknesses influence each other.

There is some overlap in each category. For example, motivation might change depending on how well I'm equipped for sharing my faith in a certain situation.

Wouldn't it be nice if a + or a - would really define our strengths and weaknesses? It is more accurate to say that each category represents a continuum rather than something we have or don't have. Motivation, for example, goes up and down depending on whom I'm talking to.

People are far more complicated than a chart. This is just a working picture.

Chart 1

Motivated	Available	Equipped	Evangelism diagnosis
-	-	-	Sequestered
-	+	-	Apathetic
-	-	+	Academic
+	-	-	Frustrated
-	+	+	Daunted
+	-	+	Isolated
+	+	-	Reckless
+	+	+	Engaged

Step Three: Now match your diagnosis to chart 2 (p. 41) to get a sketch of a basic prognosis and treatment for your growth in evangelism.

I've divided each section into six parts:

Diagnosis: From chart 1

View of Evangelism: A person's outlook on sharing the faith

Symptoms: What the diagnosis means for most

Type: A description of who this person may be

Prognosis: How this person's evangelistic efforts
or Christian life may look if left untreated

Treatment: A prescription for change and growth

Chart 2

Diagnosis: *Sequestered* **View of Evangelism:** Not interested **Symptoms:** Faith is adopted rather than personal **Type:** Cultural Christian—completely isolated from the secular world **Prognosis:** Marginalized Christian life **Treatment:** Make a commitment of faith apart from the Christian subculture.	**Diagnosis:** *Apathetic* **View of Evangelism:** "My religion is a personal thing." **Symptoms:** Sleeping giant of the church world; no functional difference from non-Christians in the workaday world **Type:** Churchgoer who does not see evangelism as important **Prognosis:** Assimilation by the secular world **Treatment:** Embrace your faith and come to know Christ's love for others; look at what the Bible says about sharing with others.
Diagnosis: *Frustrated* **View of Evangelism:** Confused by what to say and who to say it to **Symptoms:** Has a heart to share Christ **Type:** Many church members **Prognosis:** Debilitating guilt **Treatment:** Look for a mature Christian role model, learn a biblical approach to evangelism and build bridges to the secular world. Read this book!	**Diagnosis:** *Academic* **View of Evangelism:** Sees evangelism as an intellectual exercise **Symptoms:** Knows the gospel and sociological trends; doesn't know a non-Christian **Type:** Cloistered Christians **Prognosis:** Treating non-Christians as a problem or project **Treatment:** Pray for love; take concrete actions to build bridges to the secular world.
Diagnosis: *Daunted* **View of Evangelism:** Frightening or tiresome **Symptoms:** In a strong position: knows the secular world and basics of the gospel; lack of motivation hinders efforts **Type:** The fearful or burned-out; many full-time Christian workers **Prognosis:** May share out of guilt or obligation **Treatment:** Dare to share.	**Diagnosis:** *Reckless* **View of Evangelism:** Exciting job to be done **Symptoms:** Motivation and contact with the secular world give real potential; may support manipulative evangelistic schemes **Type:** Excited new Christians **Prognosis:** Sharing false things about the Christian life **Treatment:** Become equipped by developing a biblical approach to the secular world. Know the job description presented in this chapter.
Diagnosis: *Isolated* **View of Evangelism:** Wants to share, but has five church potlucks this week **Symptoms:** Could engage the world, but doesn't know non-Christians on a social basis **Type:** Busy church workers **Prognosis:** Missing the action **Treatment:** Gain an audience; become available. Take steps to make friends with a non-Christian.	**Diagnosis:** *Engaged* **View of Evangelism:** Giving away the faith **Symptoms:** Shares the gospel effectively, using a biblical approach; available to people who do not know Christ; motivated by love **Type:** All types **Prognosis:** Good (but watch out for pride) **Treatment:** Keep following Christ.

As I look around, there seem to be a lot of people who are in desperate need to hear the Christian message. They're going over the dam, as it were. So get ready for a rescue. Make sure you don't confuse your job description with the Holy Spirit's. Figure out the things that need to happen for you to become an engager of the world around you. Make yourself available, equipped and motivated. We'll see more of what that means in the next chapter.

A couple of years ago I heard they blew up the dam in my hometown. There aren't any more deaths from the dam. It's rubble on the bottom of the Ohio River. Someday this world will end, too, but until then our heavenly Father will continue to use us to rescue his lost children.

Questions for Reflection or Discussion

1. How is Mack's river rescue much like our heavenly Father's rescue of sinners?

2. How did Mack confuse job descriptions?

3. Do the chart exercise on pages 39-40.

Pray that God will make you an "engager" of your world by helping you put together the three areas of the evangelism job description.

• Four •

What I Did
on My
Spring Break:
A Study
of Engagement

Leeann and I married during our last semester of school. As active student leaders in our campus Christian fellowship, Inter-Varsity, we attended most camps and conferences they held. That April, during spring break, we traveled to InterVarsity's Fort Lauderdale beach project.

Our trip was not your ordinary college rite of spring (suds, sun, surf, sex, sand, et cetera ad nauseam). This was a Christian evangelism conference. Evangelism was more than a topic of conversation. I-V actually expected us to *do* evangelism . . . to share the gospel . . . on the beaches . . . with the revelers. Crazy, huh?

An amazing thing happened there for me. Not because this kind of evangelism is a great way to witness (talking to strangers about faith is a lousy way to see people become Christians), not because I think I did well there (I'm mildly embarrassed now about some of my attitudes), and not even because of the excellent training we received (which is the best reason to hold these kinds of projects), but because God pulled together the ideas of being available, equipped and motivated in one place—the beaches of Florida. The whole trip was different from what I planned.

I saw the week as an opportunity to finish my obligation to evangelism in a matter of days. Bite-the-bullet and hit-the-beaches. A spiritual Normandy invasion. Besides, I figured we'd learn something, since our staff promised a great speaker.

Leeann and I drove south to meet all those people we were sure to lead to Christ.

Available

Our hotel sat right on the beach and butted up to the most popular bar. The lobby reeked from that musty vomit and beer-in-the-rug smell that came from innumerable beer busts. As one reveler told me, "This place is party central." The I-V staff greeted us at the hotel, but they seemed frightened.

The beach itself was a zoo—all those almost-naked people. Muscle men strutted and bikinied women sunned while others gawked at the tanned, oiled flesh. Everyone's sound system roared loudly enough to drown out the noise of the surf. Walking down the beach was like running the tuner across the FM band of a gigantic radio.

Advertisers were everywhere. Glow-in-the-dark Frisbees touted Camel cigarettes. Roller skaters handed out handbills for sub sandwiches. Jugglers tossed trinkets to the crowds. Low-flying planes dragged banners across the sky, hawking bars and wet T-shirt contests. Even the ocean was commercialized. Boats hoisted lighted signboards and plied the waves. One bouncing light board flashed, "Come to Happy Hour at Carnivals To-night!!!!!!!" *You mean there's another carnival besides this?* I wondered.

I wasn't sure if my bedazzlement came from the broiling sun or the overstimulation of my nerves. Then it dawned on me: "I'm supposed to share the gospel with them!"

I felt I was trying to invade Normandy in a rowboat with a squirt gun. My bravado, so helpful in getting me to the beach, evaporated. I felt daunted, then ill. For a moment I thought my stomach would add its own touch to the lobby carpet.

Things I Learned About Availability

Availability—mental and physical—is the first step of evangelism. Christians need to go physically and mentally into all the world: to Africa and non-Christian cubicles at work, to Congress and smoking sections of restaurants, even to Florida beaches.

Availability does mean to go where the action is, but the real world is intimidating. It can cause us to retreat to safer grounds. When we do, we become part of a common Christian hazard: isolation. If our culture continues its move from a post-Christian to an anti-Christian society, it will be even more tempting to retreat into the warmth of a Christian subculture. But exclusive Christian fellowship isolates us from the very people who desperately need Christ. Believe me, I understand the temptation. When I got control of my case of butterflies in that hotel lobby, I thought about getting in my car and going home.

My fears made me want keep my distance and throw things at the crowd, like the jugglers on the beach. *Better yet,* I thought, *I'll rent a plane and buzz the beaches with gospel verses.* I saw John 3:16 as a vast improvement over ads for wet T-shirt contests, but not exactly what the staff had in mind.

Gimmicks remove us from having contact with real people.

God was not calling me to buzz the beach from the security of an airplane cockpit. God was calling me to meet live people on the beach.

Availability means more than *being* where the action is. Being available is also a state of mind. Christians rub shoulders with non-Christians in their workaday world all the time but keep their faith a secret. They are mentally isolated. Perhaps you've heard it said, "I witness by my actions." That is crucial, but to never speak about our hope in Christ makes people think that it's we who are great, not Jesus. Being available involves a mental decision to be open about our faith as opportunities arise.

Being available doesn't mean you have to be a wet beach towel. We did fun things. We built huge sand castles and people asked us if they could help. We organized volleyball games. We even hosted a party of our own at the hotel. Everyone was there to meet people, and it's not like you had a lot to do, so talking to new people wasn't all that strange. Sure, some were cranky, but with ten thousand hangovers, what do you expect?

The staff reminded us that Jesus often was in the thick of raucous parties because he had come to be a part of our world. When accused of hanging with the party crowd, Jesus responded, "It is not the healthy who need a doctor, but the sick" (Mt 9:12). (Sounds as if Jesus knew all about the results of beer busts.)

One staffworker, Bobby, summed it up: "You think becoming a part of the beach scene is crazy—just think about a king making his grand entrance to his kingdom in an animal stall."

Jesus said, "As the Father has sent me, I am sending you" (Jn 20:21). We are to go into the world in the way Jesus came to the world. Jesus said, in essence, "I did it and you watched, so now you do as I did." So we ask, "What did Jesus do?"

He got into our world. Bobby was right. Jesus started in an animal stall and ended on a cross (Phil 2:6-8). Jesus was God, but he got into our skin. Literally. He didn't do this out of a desire to feel pain or to look noble. He did it because our need was best met by his becoming a man. In love, we must become a part of other people's worlds. This is the basic principle of what the staff called "incarnational evangelism."

Take a risk; put yourself where the action is. For some excellent ideas about how you can be involved, read *50 Ways You Can Reach the World* by Tony Campolo and Gordon Aeschliman (IVP). Make a mental commitment of friendship to those around you who don't know Christ. Ask yourself, "Do I have a friendship with one person who does not know Christ for whom I can pray?"

Think about doing a "2 PLUS" program of prayer and action for non-Christian friends. The 2 PLUS program is a way to get started in evangelism. (See appendix one.)

Equipped

When I talked with people on the beach I realized how woefully inadequate it was to just spew out a gospel outline. I came to the project expecting to "do evangelism" all day. But the staff expected us to use our minds, not just our mouths.

Steve, a staffworker from Atlanta, strummed his guitar while perched on a folding table. His sandy toes twitched as he tutored me: "Anybody with a brain in his head is going to question our audacious claims of Christ." Steve pointed both of his palms at me, fingers down, opened his owl-like eyes wide and asked, "I mean, we claim this guy rose from the dead. What are you going to say, Mack?" Good question, I thought.

Becky Pippert was our speaker. She outlined what it meant to tell our message naturally. "How do people who have never heard the gospel relate to religious words?" she asked. "How do we approach people—people who are here to party, not to have theological discussions—with integrity? How does this relate to our life back on campus?" More good questions.

We came up with answers to good questions. We talked about answers to bad questions. We role-played in our small groups. We studied the booktable crammed with books about biblical foundations of evangelism, thoughtful apologetics, and structures for engaging the world with the gospel. It's amazing what fear will do for getting equipped.

We prayed. Boy, did we pray. We took a three-hour personal prayer time on the second day we were there. We prayed in our small groups for our time on the beach. We prayed for our prayer partners. We prayed for those we met: students, street people, dirty old men with binoculars. We prayed about lust—our own (I remember Brian confessing that every time he bowed his head to pray he saw only bikini bottoms). We prayed for the lifeguards, and the weather, and the hotel workers, and . . . you get the idea—it's amazing what fear will do for your prayer life.

We watched the Bible unfold before us as staff outlined foundations for evangelism in the whole of Scripture. I thought the New Testament contained the only insights on evangelism. I remember my amazement as I listened to a staffworker describe God's evangelistic plans starting with Genesis.

And then the staff did something very important. It was perhaps the most important thing. They went with us. They actually went on the beach and shared with us. These were not people lecturing us from the safety of a television tube or a large oak pulpit. They engaged others with us.

Things I Learned About Being Equipped

Being equipped means using our minds. Knowing a summary of the gospel is a good start. Yet equipping ourselves takes *more* than memorizing a gospel outline. We must use more of our minds. The Bible requires us to give *reasons* for the hope within us.

Being equipped means understanding the secular mindset. Study trends. Think what the Bible has to say about events in our world. Our ignorance of the secular world around us weakens our credibility to non-Christians.

And equipping ourselves goes beyond our minds. It's more than academic. Being equipped means learning by doing.

Joan and I were in a conversation with two guys on the beach. Joan was on staff in New Jersey. She weighed maybe ninety pounds. The conversation was interesting, but then they sprung my old nemesis: "We don't go to church because of all the hypocrites there."

Oh no, I thought, *just like Aspen, Colorado. We're doomed.*

Joan didn't skip a beat. "I know," she said, "it's awful. I mean, ever since I discovered the real thing I can't imagine why anyone would want to fake it."

"Real thing?" they queried. You could have picked my jaw up off the sand. "Of course," she said, with a twinkle in her eye, "you guys must have a hard time going to college since there's so many hypocrites there." She smiled. They smiled.

"Tell me the truth," she asked, "have you always done everything you felt was right?" Wow, she was on the offensive, without being offensive. She pinned those guys right to their beach mat. I was impressed. So were they. When they acknowledged their own inability to live up to everything they thought right, she mentioned, "Well, I guess hypocrites are everywhere, but there's hope for those of us who aren't perfect. God engineered a rescue for us through his Son." She said all this with engaging grace. I learned more in that one team encounter than in years on my own.

Being equipped involves prayer. Does that sound too simple?

I'm amazed how easy it is to launch an evangelistic effort and forget to pray. That tells us something about ourselves, doesn't it? Evangelism is not an exercise of information transfer where we transfer data from one hard drive to the next. Evangelism is a spiritual struggle for hearts. Hearts change only through an act of the Spirit. We need the power of God more than anything else, in evangelism. The real work of evangelism happened through those prayers we prayed on the beach—and it will happen as you begin to pray for your friends who need Christ. It's no accident that each chapter of this book concludes with a prayer.

Get Equipped

Being equipped means using our head by knowing what the Bible says (and what it doesn't say). Here are some steps you can take:

1. Start by memorizing a gospel outline. The one I memorized in the car on the drive to the beach was the same outline I shared with my sister years later to introduce her to Christ. It's called First Steps to God and is included in this book as appendix two.

2. Do more than just memorize—*study* the gospel. Ask questions about it. Understand it in your own words, live it, breathe it . . . it's far richer and deeper than we can imagine. This helps us develop a gospel worldview and frees us from canned approaches to people. Become a student of the Bible. Evangelism does start with Genesis and flows through each book of the Bible. Understanding that makes evangelism more central to our faith and less crazy.

3. Study apologetics—answers to both good and bad questions. More important, in our day and age, understand the "whys" behind tough questions.[1]

4. Become a student of your newspaper. Being equipped includes thinking through current issues "Christianly."

5. Learn by doing. Find one or more mature Christians who are actively sharing their faith and pick their brains. Better yet, find ways to involve yourself with them in evangelism.

6. Finally, ask God to work in the hearts of those around you. Do more than just pray for those around you. Pray that God will send someone your way who is a real seeker, and pray that you will have the wherewithal to respond, gently and respectfully, with reasons for the hope you have within you.

Motivated

A mix of obedience and some less pure motives drove me to the beach. That's not a bad place to start. If you're waiting for absolutely pure motives you won't do any evangelism. But it's more than obedience, much more. Right motivation for evangelism is nurtured and "grown" by our loving God.

To me, right motivation seemed harder than being available and getting equipped. The evaporation of my bravado seemed a natural result of the overwhelming glare of the beach. All that glitz made me feel outnumbered and skinny. I wanted to be obedient—just obedient in another way (say, like an all-day quiet time on a beach towel).

The mechanics of being available or getting equipped are not difficult if you're willing. Getting motivated is different. Think of it this way. Availability is moving our feet. Equipping is training our minds. Motivation is changing our hearts. Telling someone to "be motivated" is like telling someone to "be happy." It usually just makes things worse. That's because motivation is not something you do but (like happiness) a byproduct of something else.

The three things that produce right motivation are simple—at least simple to write. Right motivation for evangelism springs from love, truth and hope—and those are things we *can* work at building into our lives. Here's how I saw it work out on the beach.

Love

When we develop our relationship with God, just as we would in any deep relationship, we see his heart. We see what he loves and hates. We come to know what pleases and hurts him. We feel his passions and concerns. What is it that touches God's heart? Well, in a word, people. We are on his heart, all of us.

On the beach I started praying, "Lord, give me your heart. Let me see the beach through your eyes." That's a risky prayer for would-be evangelists, since everyone on the beach was a desperately loved child.

I started seeing the people on the beach not as the enemy but as victims—victims in need of a rescue. I found myself wondering what their real hurts and problems and dreams were. I began to wonder if parents or friends prayed for them. I wanted to let them know about the One who loved them.

I was no longer motivated by some great evangelistic technique or head of evangelistic steam fired by wanting to score points with other Christians—or even by raw obedience. It was God giving me his heart for lost people.

Paul said he tried to persuade people because Christ's love compelled him (2 Cor 5:14). When we come to know the love of God, we want to share our faith.

Sometimes in the midst of our struggles about evangelism we forget that the most loving thing we can do for people is to introduce them to Christ. Please, I am not saying don't feed hungry people. Christ intimately joined his message with acts of compassion. We must learn to do the same, while remembering that Christ alone satisfies ultimate longings.

Truth

"Jesus is a fact of history," the staff repeated, "not just something I believe." To say that Jesus is just-what-I-believe makes him no bigger than a little village idol, and that strips away all desire to tell others about him. Jesus is *the* truth, for all people, at all times, in all places. The staff told us, "If Jesus is the Truth, he will stand up in the marketplace of ideas." That made sense to me. Jesus was not true everywhere but at the beach. He is the Truth or he is not; there's no room for middle ground. Jesus *is* a fact of history. If the glitz of the beach didn't make him less true, why did he *seem* less true on the beach and (conversely) more true in church? I puzzled over this distance between Christ and beach.

Sociologists call my beach perception the effects of the plausibility structure of the culture.[2] That is, given certain settings, the gospel will appear more or less true (plausible).

When confronted by "lower plausibility structures" such as cranky neighbors, hostile professors, sneering coworkers—the beaches of our world—it's easy to forget that Jesus is the Truth. We begin to think our message is small and insignificant. That is a lie as false as the glitz of the beach. Jesus is more true than suburbs, jobs and universities all whirled into one.

At the beach, as we prayed, talked and looked at the Bible, a reversal happened in my heart. I started asking, in effect, *What does God think about the plausibility of the beach?* It made more sense to say I don't believe in all this glitz—I don't believe it offers anything that lasts except sexually transmitted diseases and skin cancer. I saw that the beach offered a very low plausibility structure to Jesus, the One who ultimately matters.

My belief in the reality of Christ and my unbelief in the reality of "the beach" motivated me to share the gospel. The truth of Christ lifted my bedazzlement. I wanted to penetrate people's worlds with the good news *because it was true.* Peter said it this way: "We did not follow cleverly invented stories when we told you about the power and coming of our Lord Jesus Christ" (2 Pet 1:16).

Today, I fear that many Christians act as though their God is just a village idol—true for their private world but not for the entire world. The truth of Christ sets us free from this small-mindedness and gives us right motivation to share the gospel.

Hope

An exciting thing happened the third day on the beach. Really exciting. A guy gave his life to Christ. I was stunned. He was from Rutgers. He told us his (long) story the third night of the project. I remember his excitement. The other details escape me, but by the end of the week other new believers had joined him. I had almost forgotten that was why we had come.

After the two motivational principles of love and truth, it's important to remember our hope. People *will* give their life to Christ. Sharing our faith brings about changed lives! The gospel has the power to change people's hearts. As Paul said, "I am not ashamed of the gospel, because it is the power of God for the salvation of everyone who believes" (Rom 1:16). Some will respond to the message with gladness and joy.

Sometimes we miss the wonder of this event. Have you ever thought about happenings on earth that are noticed in heaven? I suspect that few of the events to which we give grand and glorious coverage get much press in heaven. But when someone turns to Christ, that's different: there is locomotion in heaven. Few events here on earth make heaven rock and roll; this is one of them. "There will be . . . rejoicing in heaven over one sinner who repents" (Lk 15:7). Our hope in one person turning to Christ with joy is worth all the raised eyebrows in the world.[3]

By the end of the week someone else had changed—me. It didn't happen all at once, and I was unaware of it at the time. But it happened. Though our message seemed insignificant and a bit ridiculous, given the setting, I felt motivated to tell the people on the beach that Jesus offered more than Fort Lauderdale ever could. God changed me.

Becoming Engagers of Your World

Leeann and I didn't lead anyone to Christ that week. But many sun worshipers we talked to were keenly interested. Who knows what God did through those conversations? Leeann and I arrived at the beach hoping to finish our obligation to evangelism for a year or two. We left with a framework to engage our world—available, equipped and motivated.

That's a call for all Christians. You may not live it out in a dramatic setting like the beach of Fort Lauderdale. It may just be through one-on-one contact at work, in your dorm or in your neighborhood. Wherever it is, take a risk, work on the three foundations and engage your world.

I still go to I-V's beach project. It's at a different beach in a different city now. The crowd seems just as rowdy and the I-V students just as scared. The beach doesn't scare me anymore; I find my fears are in other places now. I even took my four-year-old son, David, when I spoke at the beach project last year. It was the tail end of biker week (Harleys, not Schwinns). David's presence gave me unbelievable opportunities to share about Christ . . . but that's another story.

Questions for Reflection or Discussion

1. In what ways is availability more than knowing non-Christians?
2. In what ways is equipping more than memorizing a gospel outline?
3. In what ways is motivation more than a head of evangelistic steam?

Ask God to give you his heart for people who don't know him.

• Five •

Speaking of Jesus

Oh, I blew it, I blew it, I blew it!" came my sister's wail of despair through my phone.

"Slow down, Linda," I said. "Blew what?"

"Oh, I blew it with Nancy . . . she asked me what I believed now, and I started telling her all kinds of stuff besides what's important."

"Hmm," I said, "like what?"

"Oh, like developing Christian values in our lives. Then Nancy started talking about the religious right, and I don't know anything about the religious right, and . . ."

"Well, that doesn't sound completely unimportant," I said, trying to be helpful.

". . . and I was just so nervous, you know how I've been praying for Nancy, and here it is and I blow it. When I was

---

walking home from her apartment I could have kicked myself."
She paused for air.

"Hmm," I repeated.

"Mack, I didn't say anything about Jesus."

My sister Linda is growing in her faith. She did many things
right with Nancy. She's now motivated to share her faith, though
she's a person who would never be accused of shoving something down someone's throat.

She's available to Nancy, even to the point of attending a New
Age seminar with her, just so she would be involved in Nancy's
world. (Linda reported the seminar was scary.)

Linda is gracious and fun. She's humble and thoughtful. But
she was right: just like many people who are starting to share
their faith for the first time, she didn't talk about what was
important. Linda garbled the gospel.

It was an opportunity missed. Not that she hadn't done some
things very well, and not that she won't have other opportunities
to speak of Jesus with Nancy.

What Happened?
Just as it would be unthinkable for a newscaster or a company
representative or a diplomat to get his or her message garbled,
so it is unthinkable for Christians to garble their message. But
Christians often feel stumped when they are asked simple
questions about basic beliefs.

Why? Most often because we don't know where to start. It's
as if someone just asked us to explain how to invest in the bond
market or the rules to Australian football.

An Evangelistic Method
Okay, I've made it clear that I am not a fan of techniques and
methods of sharing the gospel. Yet I realize we must start

somewhere. Besides, to say "don't use a method" becomes a method in itself.

Let's ask the question, What is a biblical method for sharing the gospel?

In *Evangelism and the Sovereignty of God*, J. I. Packer studies Paul's method of evangelism. He notes that no matter where Paul was—in the synagogue or the streets, in a crowd or with one person—Paul *taught* the gospel.[1]

Packer comments that Paul's method was the teaching method. Paul refers to his own ministry as a task of instruction (Eph 3:8). He did it in various ways. He often selected core elements of the message to speak about. He would analyze each element point by point, and he would explain, reason and persuade until the listeners got the message (or beat him up).

"Clearly, in Paul's view, his first and fundamental job as a preacher of the gospel was to communicate knowledge—to get gospel truth fixed in [people's] minds. To him, teaching the truth was the basic evangelistic activity; to him, therefore, the only right method of evangelism was the teaching method."[2]

May I ask a question? Can you teach the gospel? I'm not looking for teaching certificates in evangelism. But do you know how to walk someone through the basic elements of the Christian message?

My sons are playing T-ball right now. It's a delightful game . . . for the parents. Tristan, our six-year-old, seems more interested in the dandelions in the outfield.

The point of T-ball is to help kids develop some baseball skills, not play great ball. The baseball is not thrown to the batter but set on a pole at the batter box. The kids are given three swings at the stationary ball. The ball is replaced if one of the kids hits the pole instead of the ball.

The skill that this develops is a level swing. You can't play in the majors if you don't have a level swing. You can't play in the majors with a T either. The T just helps train a skill. That's what I think about a lot of methods and techniques. They help us take our first swings with the gospel. So get a copy of Romans Road, the Four Spiritual Laws, the Evangelism Explosion outline or First Steps to God, and learn how to use it. Many have made their first steps to Christ through these outlines.

But be ready to move on. These things are just tools. They aren't perfect or even complete; the gospel takes a lifetime to figure out. Remember, the goal is not to know Romans Road backwards and forwards. The goal is to know the *gospel* so well that you are able to teach its truth in your own words. Then you can teach with understanding and compassion for people's situations. That's playing in the majors.

My friend David is a quiet evangelist. Though softspoken and almost shy, David consistently shares his faith with the people around him.

His meeting with Zack is typical. Zack came to a church function with a friend, and David invited Zack to grab some lunch together the following day.

Over lunch, it became clear to David that Zack had never taken the step to give his life to Christ. Here's what David did.

David talked with Zack about his family, his job and the church function—nothing deep. Zack was intrigued with David's comments about faith. Toward the end of the time together, David fished out a copy of First Steps to God from his briefcase. First Steps to God is a simple summary of the gospel broken down into sections: God, People, Christ, Response, Cost. Each section has Scripture references. David folded it inside a Bible and gave both to Zack with these instructions: "I want you to go over this outline. Look up every reference in the Bible. Write down the meaning of each reference in your own words. Let's get together again next week and talk about what you think."

That's it. That's all David did. David taught the gospel. There was no manipulation. No offer that was untrue ("You want all your needs met, don't you?"). Most of all, David was trusting God to work in Zack's life. That's hard sometimes, but remember, Jesus dissuaded more people than he persuaded to follow him. We must never forget that it is God working in people's hearts.

The following week Zack met David for lunch again. He told David he had never thought about those Bible verses before. The love and forgiveness of God touched him, he said.

"Any questions?" David asked.

"No," said Zack.

This seems too easy, said David to himself. He decided to walk Zack through the section about the cost of making a commitment to Christ. Then he asked Zack if he wanted to pray a prayer of commitment right there. Zack started to get tears in his eyes and said, "Sure." It was full lunch-hour traffic in the restaurant. David asked if Zack wanted to go outside. "No," said Zack, "right here is fine." (Zack felt more comfortable with the crowds than David did.) David prayed a simple prayer. Zack repeated it.

Zack, now an active leader at his church, points to David's simple teaching method as the reason he is now a believer.

What Is the Core Message?

There's another reason why my sister Linda felt undone by her friend Nancy's question. Linda felt unsure about the core message of the gospel. Sometimes we are so focused on the objections and social hurdles we face that we're caught off guard by a simple question of genuine curiosity.

We need to be ready with an answer to the simple questions. They are often the most important ones.

Let me ask you another question. If someone asked you what

you believed, could you answer in clear and simple language?

First, I find it helpful to remember what the gospel *isn't*. The gospel message is not about:

- ☐ TV evangelists
- ☐ Evolution
- ☐ Family values
- ☐ The guy with weird hair and a Scripture sign at football games
- ☐ What's fair and what's not
- ☐ Speaking in tongues
- ☐ ACOA
- ☐ Republicans or Democrats
- ☐ Any of the various sins committed by Christians in the past
- ☐ Mistakes in the Bible
- ☐ The New Age
- ☐ How a good God could do one thing or another
- ☐ Amy Grant
- ☐ Cults
- ☐ Predestination
- ☐ The religious right or left

Please understand, I am not saying that we can't talk about the things on this list. Some of these things (like Amy Grant) make for interesting discussions. It may be important to talk about some of the things on this list (such as sins committed by Christians in the past) to clear up objections to faith in Christ. We'll talk about how to do that in chapters eleven and twelve.

But I am saying that when someone asks us what a real Christian is or believes, this list is off limits. We need to be ready to teach the core tenets of our faith. We can't do that if we don't have what's core and what's circumference fixed in our minds.

Add this mental check. When you find yourself discussing a

topic from the above list—or hundreds like it—ask yourself, "Does this clear the air so we can talk about core Christian beliefs, or is it circumference talk?"

The gospel message *is* about:

☐ God and his view of our condition

☐ Jesus and what he did

☐ Our personal response to God's view of us and Christ's work

God

Here is a way you might make core statements about God:

God is our Creator. He is perfect. He is perfect in his love, which he desires to lavish on us. But he is also perfect in his justice, which burns with white-hot rage at anything evil.

God perceives us in two ways. We are loved by him, passionately, deeply, perfectly. We are people created in God's image for a relationship with God. But we are also corrupted by evil and have fallen out of relationship with God.[3]

Rarely do I find people disagreeing with the idea that God is love. And most people would agree that something has gone wrong with our society and people in general. It seems people are agreeing with G. K. Chesterton, who said, "Certain new theologians dispute original sin, which is the only part of Christian theology which can really be proved."[4]

But to talk about *personal* sin raises hackles. Our culture is at odds with the word *sin*. (Which, of course, is a proof for the point.)

Nowadays people judge themselves by motive rather than action, though, curiously, when it comes to others we look at their actions and forget motive altogether. So people prefer to describe their behavior as "dysfunction" or "genetic disorder" or "boo-boo"—anything but "my sinfulness."

So when we talk about sin it's helpful to use other words than *sin*. Words like *twisted, broken* and *evil* can be helpful. The point is for us to be able to talk about sin in ways that people can identify with. For instance, I'll often say, "Most major religions agree that we're in trouble and need help."

Mark Dever, a grad student at Corpus Christi College, walked through the busy, narrow streets of Cambridge, England.

"Sir, could I interest you in some literature?" said a Hare Krishna disciple on the street corner. He pointed some books and pamphlets at Mark's midsection. His offer was made in the tone of a fast-food server: "Welcome to McDonald's, may I take your order."

Mark replied, "No, thank you."

"Why not?" asked the persistent Hare Krishna.

"Honestly?" said Mark, with raised eyebrows and a smile.

"Yes."

"Well, I think that what you're asking me to read just isn't true." Mark, still smiling, waited for the response.

"True? How can you say that?" the Hare Krishna said with a half laugh.

"Well," said Mark, "for example, I believe that Jesus was God."

"Oh, well, I do too," he replied, with a dismissive wave of the hand.

"No, no," said Mark. "You believe that Jesus was god in a Hindu sort of way. You know, in the sense that I'm god, you're god, the trees are god . . but I believe that Jesus of Nazareth was God with a capital *g*, the big one—God Almighty."

"Oh," said the Hare Krishna, with sudden awareness and concern written on his face.

Mark continued, "But don't be worried. I suspect that if most people watching us didn't know you were the Hare Krishna and I was the Christian, they would agree with you and not me."

"What do you mean?" The Hare Krishna guy's demeanor became real but cynical. Even he had a hard time seeing how a shaved-headed guy on the street corner passing out literature could be considered status quo.

Mark rubbed his chin. "Well," he began, squinting his eyes thoughtfully at the young man, "I suspect you believe that most people are created basically good and that if we just do some things right we can become better people."

"Yes, I guess that is what I believe."

"And I would suspect that most of the people walking by on this street believe that we're basically good and just need to not make mistakes to be better."

"Okay," he said as he looked around.

"But you see, I believe that we're bad, corrupted and basically rotten to our core, and that the only hope for us is radical surgery: for God to rip out our evil hearts and give us new ones. The Bible calls that being born again."

The Hare Krishna guy gave a thoughtful look. He glanced from side to side. "Umm, you wouldn't happen to have any Christian literature, would you?"

Straightaway Mark took him to a bookstall and bought him his first Christian book.

Jesus

We've got to be careful not to overspiritualize the name *Jesus*. I have heard some Christians talk about how they brought up the name *Jesus* with a friend or in a group and, magically, you could see a visible response in a crowd or on a person's face.

Well, often what is registered is social discomfort not spiritual conviction. The same reaction could happen to someone who breezed into a funeral dressed in a hot pink tutu. Some feel that to talk about any deeply held emotional topic is out of line, be it racial, political or religious.

Still, there seems to be something powerful about the name of Jesus. If you can pick only one thing to say about Christianity, speak of Jesus. Jesus is the core of our faith.

Speaking of Jesus is easy. Most people hold respect for Jesus. I rarely hear Jesus spoken of in a negative way—contrasted with, say, the TV evangelists.[5] Yes, there is a great deal of ignorance and conjecture about who Jesus was—a great moral teacher, just a Jewish rabbi, an alien from outer space. But don't take offense; use it as an opportunity. People are fascinated with Jesus, and they should be. He is fascinating! Most who have at least a passing knowledge of what he did and said are drawn to him—for good or ill.

In *Why Should Anyone Believe Anything at All?* Jim Sire says:
Put simply, the best reason for believing that the Christian religion is true is Jesus, and the best reason for believing in Jesus is Jesus himself. That may sound strange. How can Jesus be a reason? . . . Christianity, it turns out, is fundamentally about a person—the person of Jesus. Christianity proclaims that God has made himself known in many ways—through the Hebrews, through the events of history, through the shape and form of the universe itself, through visions and personal encounters with God. But he has most supremely made himself known in and through Jesus Christ.[6]

Here's a way you might make some core statements about Jesus:
God's love is the reason that he longs for us. God's justice is the reason that we all face eternal separation from him. I call this the cosmic dilemma. The solution—the only solution—comes from God himself. He sent his Son, Jesus, to live the perfect life.
Jesus was fully man and fully God. The primary aim and

work of his life was to pay the penalty for our evil nature. He did that by allowing his life to be taken through an execution on a cross. Though Jesus was a man of miracles, one miracle stands above all others—Jesus rose from the dead. Now, because of his execution and resurrection, Jesus rules the spiritual world, and one day he will be the judge of the physical world.

Response

Finally, we must be ready to say that Jesus requires response. It has been said that all generations must decide what they are to do with Jesus. So must all individuals who hear about him.

Andy, a high-school teacher, shook his head and laughed. "You know, Mack, I never thought I'd say this, but Jesus makes sense to me now. I've been learning stuff about faith that's got my head spinning. It's almost like Jesus has been talking to me—you know—personally."

"Well, Andy," I said, "maybe now is the time for you to respond by handing over your life to him."

"Yeah," Andy said, almost matter-of-fact, "it is. I'm ready."

Here's a way you might make some core statements about a response to Jesus:

Christianity is not an academic exercise. What is required is to respond. If anyone, from a choirboy to a hardened prison inmate, decides to follow Christ, the response is the same. We come to God as both our lover and our judge. We speak to him and to him alone. We tell him that we are aware of the distance between us. We tell him we desire to restore the relationship broken by our evil. (Evil can be as blatant as cheating on our spouse or as slippery as loving money or feeling pride.) Whatever it is, we tell him we are willing to do an about-face from this evil to follow him.

We tell him that we believe in his sacrifice on the cross as payment for our evil. We tell him we believe in the miracle of his resurrection. Finally we tell him we are willing to follow him, in faith, as leader of our lives in a relationship that is personal, not academic—no matter where that takes us.

Since you bear a message worth knowing, take a few minutes to study it. To say these three core statements takes about two and a half minutes. It may be the most important couple of minutes in someone's life.

Questions for Reflection or Discussion

1. As Linda began to grow spiritually, she (just like Mack) struggled with her first efforts to share her faith. Why?
2. What do you notice, in contrast, about David's time with Zack?
3. Write out, in your own words, the core tenets of the gospel.

Pray for an opportunity to talk with someone about one of these Christian basics.

• Part II •

How Jesus Engaged His World

The woman said, "I know that Messiah"
(called Christ) "is coming. When he comes, he will
explain everything to us."
Then Jesus declared, "I who speak to you
am he." (Jn 4:25-26)

• Six •

Divine Appointments

Jesus was ready for divine appointments. In fact, he was a walking divine appointment! He engaged the world around him. He was available, equipped and motivated. Jesus traveled through life with divine purpose in every step. His confident march pulled people along with him.

Jesus' clear focus on the eternal enabled him to reach across social barriers. He spoke the truth, yet his approach was humble. Jesus' interaction with the woman at the well models for us the way to become engagers of our world.

The Pharisees heard that Jesus was gaining and baptizing more disciples than John, although in fact it was not Jesus who baptized, but his disciples. When the Lord learned of this, he left Judea and went back once more to Galilee. Now he had to go through Samaria. (Jn 4:1-4)

The first verses of John 4 have gaps I long to fill. I wonder what Jesus said to the disciples on their six-hour walk[1] that morning. What was it like for Jesus to experience hunger and thirst after knowing only perfect satisfaction in heaven? The Pharisees somehow triggered Jesus' departure. They suspected his popularity would overshadow John the Baptist's.[2] Were they sowing trouble between the followers of John and Jesus? We know they wanted to kill Jesus (Jn 7:1); was he fleeing a murder plot?

One part of this section is clear. Their journey took them through the land of the Samaritans, and by noon they were deep in enemy terrain. No doubt this route unsettled his disciples.

Jews viewed the Samaritans as hated half-breeds. Samaritans' roots were Jewish, but their ancestors had intermarried with Gentiles. "Adultery!" said the Jews. Samaritans had collaborated with Gentiles during ancient wars. "Treason!" said the Jews. Samaritans claimed that the worship of God should take place on Mount Gerizim rather than in Jerusalem. "Blasphemy!" said the Jews.[3]

Bigotry toward Samaritans ran so deep that some Jews, when traveling from Galilee to Jerusalem, took their journey through rough country on the other side of the Jordan just to bypass Samaria. It took longer than the three-day walk straight through, but it kept them free from contamination.[4] Some Jews did travel through Samaria, but it was a lock-your-doors experience.

The text says Jesus *had to go* through Samaria. This was not a geographical need; many Jews took the other route. Why did Jesus have to go? Because he intended to keep an appointment, a divine appointment, with the woman at the well.

Do you want to engage your world? Are you trying to be available, equipped and motivated? Have you made a commitment to reach out to those around you? Are you praying that God will use you in evangelism? Then look for a divine appointment.

There was a point in my life when I didn't even believe in divine appointments. Now I think *all* Christian encounters have that potential.

Fasten Your Seat Belt

"Late again," I grumbled. The rush to the airport didn't feel like a rush to a divine appointment, I just felt late. "Flight 410 to Memphis is leaving in ten minutes, Mr. Stiles. If you hurry you can just make it." Sometimes ticket agents sound like my fifth-grade librarian. *Why can't I ever get to the airport on time?* I muttered to myself. *I'm always the last person on the plane.*

It didn't click that God had made my reservations even when I "happened" to meet Bill Wilkerson on the plane. Bill had attended the I-V chapter at the University of Tennessee when I worked there as the I-V staffworker. He had graduated from UT and started his first year of seminary. Ministry excited Bill.

Bill's disregard for people's opinion of him was his trademark. Joanne, another UT student, said she learned how to cut hair on Bill's head. He didn't care how the cut looked; he just wanted it out of his eyes. Not that he was bad-looking—far from it, despite his lopsided haircuts. Bill's engaging and hardy nature suited barbers. People trying to avoid attention in public places found Bill a bit loud.

We both had aisle seats. I got 17B. Bill sat in row 15 on the opposite side. Flights to Memphis from Knoxville take about an hour, and Bill didn't waste a minute. When we took our seats, he began a barrage of questions over the noise of the jet engines.

"So, Mack," he boomed across the aisle and past the folks in 16 A, B, C and D, "how's the ministry of the gospel going on campus?"

"Fine, Bill, uh, fine," I said, looking around. People glared over the tops of their papers at us—mostly at me, it seemed. I felt like a kid making too much noise in church.

"Uh, Bill, would you mind keeping it down a little? I'd hate to disturb all these folk reading their *Wall Street Journals.*"

Bill didn't hear me. "What's it like to get to serve Christ all the time, Mack?" More stares. I could just hear the other passengers: "Oh boy, a couple of religious nuts."

Bill went on, "Man, I can't wait till I'm out of seminary and serving the Lord full-time." I thought if people rolled their eyes any more they would fall out of their heads. To my dismay our plane went into a holding pattern. Bill's blitzkrieg continued.

Finally the captain announced our clearance to land. As I straightened my seat back to its fully upright position, I glanced out the window and caught the eye of the woman sitting next to me.

She smiled and said, "I couldn't help overhearing that you are a religious person."

You and everyone else on this plane, I thought to myself. Then I said, "Yes," and gave her a pitiful smile as if to say ". . . and I'm so sorry."

She said, "I've been asking lots of religious questions lately."

The seat belt warning chimed.

"Really?" I said. My face continued to look at her. But my mouth went dry; I had that pennies-on-the-tongue taste that comes with sudden awareness. God had set me up!

"Yes. See, I'm a sergeant in the Army, and this past year these religious thoughts kept coming to me, just questions, you understand, so last week I went to the chaplain and told him that I really wanted to know God. He sure did know a lot about God. Really, though, I just left confused."

The plane banked to start its approach.

"I think that's a very good distinction," I said.

"What do you mean?" she asked.

"Well, it's good to make the distinction between knowing God and knowing about God. For instance," I continued, "we know a lot about George Washington. We know what he looks like. We know what he did. We know personal things about him and his family. We even know he wore a wig."

"And wooden dentures," she said.

"Really? I didn't know that!" I said. "At any rate, we couldn't say we knew him the way Thomas Jefferson could say he knew him."

"Yes," she said.

The flight attendant reminded me to fasten my seat belt.

I said, "Well, the same is true of God. We can know a lot *about* God and still not know God."

My mouth was on autopilot. I had said this, or something similar, a thousand times on campus (at least I had learned the message). My head, though, was in a tailspin. *Please, God, forgive me for being more concerned about what people think of me than what they think of you. Forgive me for being more worried about the* Wall Street Journal *than your gospel. I'm too quick to think about my status, my clothes, my nose hairs—any stupid and trivial thing I can worry about—rather than what's important.*

"Yes, I see," she said.

The plane went into its final approach.

I said, "You know what? I think when you feel those religious questions it's God calling you to a relationship with him. Not just to get knowledge about him, but to know him as a friend."

"Oh," she said. She stared at the seat table in front of her, thinking over the call of Christ.

The wing flaps bumped down.

I said, "Do you know there is a dilemma in heaven over you?"

"How so?" she said.

"Well, God wants a relationship with us, but our broken and selfish nature blocks it. God's law demands a perfect sacrifice to break the barrier that's formed between his perfection and our selfishness." I used my hands to illustrate the barrier. "We can't do it ourselves; we're imperfect. So, God paid the penalty himself: he offered his Son. Jesus' death on the cross served as payment for our selfishness and broke the barrier to God. Jesus rose from the dead. That shows that he is the Truth. Now he offers forgiveness and opens the way for us to have a new relationship with God."

"That's what I want," she said.

I blinked as the plane bumped down on the runway. I had forgotten to fasten my seat belt.

I said, "Well, this relationship between you and God starts by your believing that Christ is the risen God, turning from self-centeredness and making your life his home by giving him control of your life. Do you feel willing to do that?"

She nodded and said, "Yup."

"I could pray with you now if you would like."

"Okay," she said.

We prayed. The chimes bonged and everyone stood up to get their stuff before the plane stopped. Since we were late, she worried about missing her connection. She shook my hand, once, military-like. She was chipper. "Thanks a whole bunch. That was really helpful."

I stared back at her, dazed. "Tell your chaplain what you've done and get a Bible—one that's in a modern translation." I was still on autopilot. "Read the book of John in your Bible first."

"John, got it. Okay, well, bye."

"Bye." I sat in my seat to let the folks catching connecting flights get off.

After a few minutes I thought to myself, *I didn't even get her name.*

"Come on, Mack, you don't want to go to Denver, do you?" I looked up and there was Bill grinning down at me. The plane was empty except for Bill and me and a flight attendant cleaning out the seat pockets. "You know what," he said with childlike wonder, "I just had the best conversation about the Lord with the guy who sat next to me." I almost gave that big lummox a kiss.

Uncomfortable? Don't Worry

We won't know the exact times, dates and places of our appointments. It's enough to know that they will happen. They may not come easy, either. Your divine appointment may be different from what you expect, it may happen with people you wouldn't choose, and it may be in a place that will surprise you. Your divine appointment may happen when you're tired, or when it's inconvenient, or when you've got other things on your mind. But it will happen.

Sometimes I wonder if the disciples didn't feel about Jesus the way I felt about Bill . . . that Jesus' reckless disregard for social etiquette landed them in situations that were uncomfortable . . . and spiritually fruitful.

The divine appointment God is arranging for you right now could be in any seat on any plane. It may be with a family member or a long-time friend. It may be with someone at the drinking fountain at work. Jesus will drag you to your appointment as surely as he dragged the disciples to Samaria. The question is, how will you respond?

Our response should follow Jesus' confident model. But his confidence and care and clear focus often escape us. Sometimes I'm so busy with myself that I lose out on what's important. I learned some valuable lessons from my encounter with that woman Army sergeant (I call her "Sarge").

Divine appointments aren't what you expect. It's easy to pigeonhole encounters with people. If I were God, someone from Officers Christian Fellowship would have sat next to Sarge, not me. I work with college students. But I'm not God, and he didn't ask me for advice. Remember, our ways aren't his ways.

What a Coincidence!

When you're praying, "Lord, use me in evangelism," be ready. Watch for it to happen.

David was having his quiet time in the student cafeteria. He prayed, "Lord, please use me in evangelism." He lifted his head to see another guy standing over him. "Excuse me," he said, "there aren't any empty tables. Could I sit by you?" Sitting down, the guy looked over at David's open Bible. "What are you reading?"

David thought, *Wow, Lord, that was quick work.*

Pray. Connect with your source. Repent, as I did, if you need to. I repented and was humbled even during my conversation with Sarge. "Sarge" came to Christ despite my self-absorption. The same self-absorption that caused the Pharisees to worry about their power base, the disciples to fret about social etiquette, and a staffworker to feel embarrassed by his boisterous friend.

Is your faith standing out, *despite* your best efforts? Don't hide. God may be setting you up. Relax and watch. This is your answered prayer. Don't be too concerned about how you look. God isn't. Just think: without Bill's confidence and Christlike focus on things eternal, plus his scorn for accepted behavior, it could have been just another flight instead of a divine appointment.

Questions for Reflection or Discussion

1. What steps did Jesus take to make a divine appointment happen?

2. What steps do you need to take—with your mind, heart or feet—to make a divine appointment happen?

Pray that God will help you be ready for an encounter he sets up.

• Seven •

Jesus Had
an Attitude

How we approach others with the gospel is just as important
as being ready for divine appointments and knowing the message. Today many evangelistic techniques and methods concen-
trate mostly on gaining the upper hand in a conversation. This
has the unfortunate result of turning any conversation into a
power play for God.

Power plays may be how *we* want to start our evangelistic
efforts, but not Jesus. Jesus didn't cause water to gush out of
the well like a giant fire hydrant. He didn't demonstrate how
he could beat the woman at the well in basketball. He didn't
offer to buy the well. Jesus' approach was not a power play
or display of magic. Jesus started with humility.

So he came to a town in Samaria called Sychar, near the plot of
ground Jacob had given to his son Joseph. Jacob's well was there,

and Jesus, tired as he was from the journey, sat down by the well. It was about the sixth hour. When a Samaritan woman came to draw water, Jesus said to her, "Will you give me a drink?" (His disciples had gone into the town to buy food.) (Jn 4:5-8)

Humility Is Not Weakness

Understand, Jesus was not a weak person. He radiated power. He calmed storms. He cast out devils. He raised the dead. But these were acts of service for others—Jesus never served *himself* with his power.[1]

Jesus modeled availability through the attitude of humility, not by wielding power. John 4 is a human picture of Jesus. It's noon, he has walked for six hours, and now he's thirsty. There's no thirst like a thirst that can see and hear water but not taste it. So he asks for help: "Will you give me a drink?"

The world's most powerful man first spoke words of humble weakness to the woman at the well. This model of humility is genius for evangelism. We can't be omnipotent, but we can be humble. After all, we don't get much practice at omnipotence.

Not that I don't try. Serving myself with power is still a potent temptation. I long to look strong and powerful, especially in evangelism. *My stunning answers to those cynics made them look ridiculous. My rosy life in Christ is without need. And yes, thanks to God, I rarely make a mistake.*

That's ridiculous, of course. My best answers to cynics are thought up after the conversation is over. I have real needs. I'm imperfect—just ask Leeann. That's all clear, but I still gravitate to power in evangelism. I want to knock 'em over for Jesus rather than be humble.

Humility Is Not Easy

Leeann and I have directed several short-term mission programs in Africa. One summer, while we were there, we experienced one of the most powerful evangelistic experiences I've ever known. And it happened because of the humility of one student, Joanne.

Students in Africa discover that Americans' global awareness ranks low. But what we lack in awareness we cover by zeal. We try harder. We want to make things happen. The most frequent question students ask on our short-term projects is, "What am I going to *do?*" We excel at doing.

"Put us to work," the students plead.

"We want to dig wells, hand out food, preach in churches," they say. "The bigger the project the better," they say. We love big projects; they make us feel powerful. If things aren't happening, we feel useless and weak. Above all we hate weakness.

That summer, an elderly African gentleman spoke to us during our orientation in Kenya. We sat in a circle around him. His soft, lilting African-English echoed in the concrete room. Though his words fell gently on our ears, they pierced my heart.

"Bwana Asafiwe" ("Praise the Lord"), he said. "I love the Lord Jesus with all my heart." This is a ritual greeting we heard often from Christians in Kenya. He said he felt nervous but honored to speak to an American group. "My parents came to Christ through missionaries from your country," he said. "The missionaries buried two of their children here. I am grateful to them for their sacrifice. I am grateful to your country for sending them." We felt tinges of pride.

Then, almost apologetically, he said, "Today, my young brothers and sisters, I fear for you." He used the podium to steady himself. "Your great strength is now your weakness. Many no longer know how to share as Jesus did, with humility, like a servant."

Humility? Like a servant?

It was hard to tell what the students heard, but I didn't think he had an impact. We don't want to hear things like that; we want to believe we're different. The old man was only one of many speakers, and we kept the students busy: we spent the rest of the week studying the book of Philippians and preparing for specific assignments.

At the end of orientation we scattered students across Kenya to live in African Christian homes. Joanne went to live with the Ndutiris.

Mr. Ndutiri worked for a youth ministry to high-school kids. Stories circulated during orientation about revival among Kenyan students. "Joanne, get ready to reap a harvest," one orientation visitor told her.

"High-school kids come to Christ in droves at every meeting," another said.

This talk excited Joanne. She had become a Christian through the ministry of Young Life in high school. She'd worked as a Young Life leader in college. This assignment had the feel of a perfect fit. She polished her testimony. She worked on a sermon. She looked forward to ushering in God's kingdom through her evangelistic efforts.

The Ndutiris' home was a typical African city home. They had running water and electricity, unlike many places where other students stayed. But they faced their share of hardships too. Joanne arrived during Mrs. Ndutiri's ninth month of pregnancy. Mrs. Ndutiri struggled to do the housecleaning, shopping and cooking along with caring for her children.

As we prepared Kenyan families for their American guests, we told them, "Our students come as servants and learners. Treat them as family, not as guests. Put them to work at what would best serve Christ." The Ndutiris took us literally. They asked Joanne to do the housework.

There's Been Some Mistake!

Housework is hard in Kenya. Joanne said later she didn't know much about housework in America, much less Kenya. Imagine doing an entire family's wash by hand. Joanne bargained at the open market for food. She scrubbed floors, laundry and kids. Joanne cleaned and cooked chicken (Mr. Ndutiri slaughtered the chicken, though he puzzled over Joanne's squeamishness). She served the meals and did the dishes. She served tea, a Kenyan custom, twice a day. Another Kenyan custom: guests streamed in for breakfast, lunch and dinner. Joanne fell into bed each evening exhausted from fumbling through foreign routines in a foreign land.

Initially Joanne bided her time until the real ministry of evangelism would start. Her first thoughts sounded more reasonable than angry. First angry thoughts always do. *I've raised a lot of money. I've come a long way. I sure hope we get to do something useful.*

The Ndutiris didn't say please and thank you either. The Ndutiris appreciated Joanne. She was a godsend for them. But Kenyans show their appreciation in other ways than saying please and thank you. These words are rarely used in Swahili. Joanne didn't know that. To her the requests sounded rude. "Joanne, fix the tea. Joanne, do the wash. Joanne, change the babies."

I'm getting a degree in nursing! thought Joanne. *Surely there is something* significant *that I could do?*

During the second week she wondered why they hadn't gone to the high schools. At first she thought Mr. Ndutiri was dragging his feet. No, Mr. Ndutiri had canceled all their engagements because the baby was due any day and Joanne had too much to do at the house to talk to high-school students. Dread fell on Joanne: three weeks . . . at the Ndutiris' . . . as the house help. *What will my supporters think when I tell them all I did on my short-term mission was clean house?* she wondered.

As Joanne's dreams for high-school evangelism fizzled, she wondered about other students' exciting adventures. She envisioned their glorious opportunities. She felt ripped off.

Toward the end of her second week she was hanging the wash on the line. She had had enough. The crushing responsibilities of a home plus the added weight of another culture boiled over.

I'm here as a guest in their home, and how do they treat me? she thought. *I'm better than this.* She stomped her foot. *Why, they're treating me like I'm the help. They just want me to be their . . . their servant.*

A servant. Suddenly it hit her—right there in an African back yard between a banana tree and a clothesline. *What was it that old man said at orientation?* And then the full force of her study in the book of Philippians punched through.

"Your attitude should be the same as that of Christ Jesus: Who, being in very nature God, did not consider equality with God something to be grasped, but made himself nothing, taking the very nature of a servant" (Phil 2:5-7).

There it was, as clear and bright as the African sky. To hang the Ndutiris' wash was to be like Jesus.

The work around the house didn't change. If anything, it was more difficult after Mrs. Ndutiri gave birth to their third child during Joanne's last week. But Joanne changed. The baby was a joy, and Joanne was now a part of the family. She finished her time with the Ndutiris with little fanfare. Joanne never became a great Kenyan evangelist, though she did make it to a couple of high schools. More important than the projects she did was her witness of servanthood.

A week later Shiro met some friends on the streets of Nairobi. Shiro, a Kenyan student, was taking part in our program. Her friends confronted her: "What are you doing with all these

Americans?" The U.S. and its people are not always loved and respected overseas.

"Oh, no," Shiro explained, "they're not like the others. Some of these people served as house help in Kenyan homes." Her friends looked flabbergasted.

The word was out. African Christians began to look at our group differently. Soon we were exploring partnerships between Kenyan university Christians and our group.

The following summer Kenyan and American students joined each other for a week-long evangelistic outreach. We journeyed to Maasai country on the edge of the Rift Valley. The outreach was the most powerful evangelistic effort I've ever known. Hundreds of people came to Christ due, in part, to the witness of American and Kenyan Christian students working together.

One night during our outreach I slipped out of my sleeping bag and took a walk under the African stars. I wondered if our outreach would have happened without Joanne. It wasn't her power that served as a witness, but her humility. Joanne did usher in God's kingdom, but it happened in a way she didn't expect. She didn't even get to see it.

I thought about stars in the Bible.

"Do everything without complaining or arguing, so that you may become blameless and pure, children of God without fault in a crooked and depraved generation, in which you shine like stars in the universe as you hold out the word of life" (Phil 2:14-16).

Of all the powerful programs and projects we did in Africa, from hunger relief to hut-to-hut evangelism, from working in clinics to preaching to high-school youth groups, none made us more available to non-Christians than an American house helper in a Kenyan home.

I'm glad Joanne got the point. She offered herself humbly, like Christ. It came with struggle, but what important thing doesn't? In the mix Joanne grew more like Jesus. That was worth the trip—no matter what her supporters thought.

Satan tempted Jesus to use his power to serve himself. The Christian culture is tempted in the same way today. Christians ask, "Why shouldn't Christians be powerful too? Let's use our power to serve our evangelistic aims." It's easy to forget Christ's humility in a powerful society. It's easy to forget that "the weapons we fight with are not the weapons of the world" (2 Cor 10:4). So evangelistic power plays flourish. Our cultural strength has become our spiritual weakness.

Beware the Power Play

I'm using "power plays" to mean false and controlling methods that trick people into making a commitment. A power play is manipulative. It glorifies marketing techniques and personalities over the Spirit's work in hearts. It misrepresents Jesus.

Whatever form power plays take, they can tempt us to forget that God's way is not through might or power or strength, but through his Spirit. Here are four checks for power plays in any of our evangelistic efforts.

1. *Avoiding power plays in evangelism is tricky.* It would be easy if certain *forms* of evangelism took the nature of a power play and others didn't. But they don't. Friendship evangelism can be manipulative and contact evangelism can be sensitive—after all, Jesus was doing contact evangelism with the woman at the well.

These methods of evangelism come and go. That's as it should be—methods aren't the gospel. Some methods today are more effective that those of yesteryear. Certain methods effective in the past seem downright corny today. Whatever method you use, make sure it starts with a humble approach.

To prevent power abuse and guard integrity in witness, a "Code of Ethics for Christian Witness" has been drawn up (see appendix three). It deals with things such as thoughtful, unpressured decision-making, appeals that bypass the mind, and so on. It will be of help as you consider approaches to use—and not use.

2. Programs have great potential for power abuse. *The biggest misuse of power in programs is hero worship.* Heroes in our culture don't give up their rights, act humble and hang on crosses. They make lots of money, play sports and look pretty. Many of these people are genuine and real Christians, but, through no fault of their own, they are "platformed" in a way that is dangerous to the message of Christ (and harmful to them personally). Be careful. Sometimes we're asking people to accept a quarterback into their heart, not Jesus.

3. There are traps to avoid when we do personal evangelism as well. In friendship evangelism, *guard yourself from trying to look perfect.* I noticed this tendency when talking to my children. My stories to our kids told them how their daddy overcame some great moral or physical problem with his prowess. I set them up to think I was so wonderful I didn't need God. Once I realized this, I started telling them stories of my mistakes and my need for Christ. Not only was this a more accurate picture of Daddy, but the stories were more interesting.

As I've mentioned, Jesus' interaction with the woman at the well was "contact evangelism"—a term for sharing the gospel with someone you don't know. "Contact evangelism" is used in contrast with "friendship evangelism." I find these descriptions confusing. Do we avoid contact in friendship evangelism? Are we unfriendly in contact evangelism? Well, at least friendship evangelism sounds friendly; contact evangelism sounds like contact football. Wham, knock 'em over for Jesus.

I propose a new movement. Let's throw out these terms altogether. Evangelism today needs humble spontaneity and give-and-take dialogue—both with friends and with strangers. Our movement's motto (with apologies to the Woodstock folks) can be "Evangelize the one you're with."

Remember, Jesus at the well is a picture of humble humanity. Share your weakness with people. God can cause our weakness to become our strength. It cuts both ways. Go to others in humility, as Jesus did. Ask for help if you need it. Let them know how Christ has made a difference despite your doubts and failures. Tell people how Christ met you in your pain and how he loved you through it. This is far more real and true than the "perfect Christian" mentality.

4. Remember that *"doing" comes naturally for North Americans and Europeans*. We often feel insecure in evangelism, and so we overcompensate by doing things. This serves to boost ourselves instead of Christ. It's natural—and dangerous.

I realize I've formed a paradox. I've called for Christians to be active in evangelism. To *do* evangelism. Then I turn around and say be careful of doing evangelism. But there is a big difference between sharing with someone about Christ and doing the busy-work that some call evangelism. Doing for the sake of doing is not Jesus' model. He didn't knock himself out setting up a living Christmas tree so he could impress the woman at the well. He just sat down and asked for a drink.

Constant doing has a narcotic effect. It gets the evangelistic monkey off our back. It makes us feel good, powerful, even euphoric, but it masks our true hurts and pains. Doing is addictive. When we stop doing we can even go through withdrawal and depression. The sad irony is that busyness sedates us and then we miss real evangelistic opportunities that come our way.

Remember, Jesus' first words to the woman at the well were

"Can you give me a drink?" Those words are similar to some of his last. On the cross he said, "I thirst." His death on the cross was the ultimate statement of humility and servanthood.

Jesus purchased freedom for the woman at the well—and for us too—through his work on the cross. Humility and vulnerability are inherent in our message, since we speak of a crucified Lord. If our evangelistic efforts look powerful or strong, they are often in contradiction with the message of the cross. Humility, not strength, is Christ's way in evangelism.

Questions for Reflection or Discussion

1. How did Jesus model humility in his interaction with the woman at the well?

2. What had to happen for Joanne to follow his example?

3. What was the result, in part, of Joanne's humility?

4. Name the four checks to guard against power plays (and foster humility) in our evangelistic efforts.

Pray that humility will mark your speech and actions as you offer the words of life.

• Eight •

Crossing Barriers

The Samaritan woman said to him, 'You are a Jew and I am a Samaritan woman. How can you ask me for a drink?' (For Jews do not associate with Samaritans)" (Jn 4:9).

"How can you ask me for a drink?" The woman at the well knew she was a social outcast. She knew Jesus' one request broke four barriers. He talked to a social outcast. He interacted across racial lines. He spoke to a woman. He requested a defiled drink. Christ crossed all of those social barriers with one simple question.

Social barriers make us comfortable. When they are in place we don't have to deal with scary people. But here's shocking news: our comfort has a very low biblical priority. Jesus doesn't seem to care much about our comfort. If anything, Jesus' call is to give up comfort. Jesus seems more interested in our getting to know scary people. Throughout the Gospels we see examples of Jesus knocking out his disciples' comfort by befriending the outcasts. He does the same for us—when we let him.

I wonder if we really grasp the scandals Jesus caused. The hatred between the Jews and the Samaritans is lost in history. We use the word only to name hospitals "Good Samaritan Hospital." But there are plenty of modern-day equivalents: think of the conflict between Jews and Arabs today. A right-wing white South African and a black member of the ANC. Protestants and Catholics in Ulster. Yet for some of us even these have a distant quality.

How about the militant lesbian spewing her hatred toward Christians in the campus newspaper? How about the glazed-eyed inner-city gang member who could care less about Jesus, the white man's God? Would Jesus visit these people? Would he know their names, go to their parties, tell them stories? He would.

And we would be shocked. "Did you hear that Jesus was at the gay/lesbian meeting last night rather than at church?" we'd say. "What is he doing hanging out with people like them?" we'd say. "Doesn't he know who he's talking to?"

It's true that we need to reach those close to us in the everyday; it is also imperative for believers to reach out to those who are wildly different.

So how do we cross these barriers? Well, Jesus *started* by asking some questions. It got things rolling.

Motorcycle Sid

Sallie, my administrative assistant, kept the office as neat as a pin. She made her own modest dresses. She drove the same car for a decade. You can imagine my shock when Sal told me she had started a friendship with a guy in a motorcycle gang.

"Strictly platonic," she reassured me. "Sid is just a friend." Then she told me they had been grocery shopping together and had a "nondate" to a movie. This was supposed to reassure me? It sounded like the fast track to marriage.

Sal had already introduced Sid to her mother (I wish I had seen that!). I fantasized about the wedding reception: lots of leather and lace, people being thrown into punch bowls, great-aunts being goosed. This just wouldn't do. I wondered how to tell Sid to get lost and leave Sal alone—without shedding my blood.

I wondered how to even talk to a motorcycle gang member. I had no clue how to start. Dad didn't let us use the word *motorcycle* in our house, so I knew nothing about them. *Maybe, I thought, I should meet him first.*

I mentioned to Sallie, "Would you mind letting Sid know I would love a ride on a Harley?"

Later that week I heard a low rumble down the street. It grew into a deafening extended explosion. Just as my office window started chattering, the noise stopped, leaving a ringing silence. Moments later, in sauntered Sid.

He looked the part. A short, oily ponytail hung limp on his neck. His unbuttoned leather vest functioned as a shirt. His naked belly hung over his wide leather belt. A brass chain fastened his fat leather wallet to a belt loop on his jeans. It jingled whenever his right foot landed on the floor, giving a metallic, peg-legged tempo to his walk. His red, purple and blue dagger tattoo further accented his modern-day pirate outfit—simply everything Sal's mom wanted for a son-in-law!

He carried two motorcycle helmets.

Motorcycle Mack?

I said, "Hi."

"Hear you like Harleys," he said, with a note of disbelief in his surprisingly high-pitched voice. He stared at my shelves filled with Christian books.

"You bet," I said.

He tossed me a helmet. I bobbled, then clutched it.

"Let's take a ride," he commanded.

"Sure," I said, wondering what I had gotten myself into.

His motorcycle was a thing of beauty. It was a chopped Harley. A chopped motorcycle (now that I'm educated) is a bike with a front wheel extended beyond the normal position. Sometimes the wheel tines are stretched the length of the motorcycle, though Sid's bike had a shorter, more reasonable chop.

The motorcycle's engine looked larger than the one in my Toyota. The airbrushed nude on the gas tank reclined tastefully beneath an airbrushed palm tree.

The passenger seat was a sort of backseat throne: from its elevated position one looked down on the driver, who seemed only inches off the pavement. There was a large "sissy bar" on the back seat—three crosses welded together. I don't think they bore any religious significance; they just kept people from falling off the passenger seat. Holding onto the sissy bar behind my back was awkward, but I thought it preferable to wrapping my arms about Sid's bare belly.

My biggest regret of the day was forgetting to take a picture. I could use it now with the kids to play "What's Wrong with This Picture?"

Motorcyclist looks right.

Chopped Harley looks right.

Who's the man in a polo shirt, shorts, tennies and a helmet emblazoned with a swastika? (I didn't look the part.)

Sid kicked the engine to life. "Where you want to go?" he yelled over the din.

Without hesitation I shouted back, "To campus. I want all the students to see me."

There are a few of life's moments stuck in my mind as fresh as if they happened yesterday. My tour around campus with Sid is one of them. I see it clearly as a video, but it's better than video: I smell the exhaust, I feel the numbness from the vibration, I sense the dissonance of Motorcycle Sid and me . . . together.

From my perch on the passenger seat, I waved to people on campus as if I was the beauty queen of a small-town parade. Sid now was enjoying my joy. He revved his engine at traffic lights.

People actually rolled up their windows and locked their doors as we pulled up. The only people who looked at us were the children. They cocked their heads and laughed. Some pointed; others pulled on their parents' collars from the back seat to get them to look. Adults didn't want to look. They gripped the steering wheel and pointed their unblinking eyes straight ahead as if they didn't notice or were uninterested. Both seemed impossible.

Their fear seemed strange to me. I wanted to reassure them, "It's just me, Mack, Christian student worker. I won't hurt you." I wanted to tell them that Sid was a very nice guy and that if they wanted he would probably give rides to their children. It was no use. Their fear was as real to them as their children's fear of something living under the bed.

"How often do you ride your Harley?" I yelled to Sid.

"Well, I really don't like riding my bike without others," he said.

"How come?" I asked.

"When you ride alone cops stop you and John Wayne you," he said.

"John Wayne you?" I asked.

"Yeah, you know, push you around, it makes 'em feel big." Suddenly Sid seemed more real.

"Gee, Sid, I'm sorry."

"No big," he said.

I had to add the "deal" in my mind.

Appreciation filled me. Sid had ridden his bike alone just to give me a ride.

Sid told me about his fondness for animals. He invited me to go fishing on the farm he owned in rural Tennessee. It didn't take a rocket scientist to figure that there were rough things about his life and his past, but it was easy to see how God loved Sid. He had hopes and fears and dreams. Sid was a nice guy.

Suddenly, Sid seemed like a real person. He needed a real relationship with Christ. God was growing in my heart a deeper sense of his love for his lost children—even motorcycle gang children. Maybe a wedding reception on his farm wouldn't be so bad anyway. If his friends were half as nice as Sid it might be fun . . .

Sid taught me a valuable lesson: asking questions helps us cross barriers. For me, Sid was a social outcast. He was scary to me at first. I felt closer to those folk rolling up their windows and locking their doors than I'd like to admit. I suppose I was a sort of motorcycle gang bigot.

No one would have thought it strange if I had told Sid to shove off. In fact, I might have been hailed a hero of American values if I had acted tough and told him to just stick to his own kind. But it would have been the end of an opportunity.

My worries about wedding bells were absurd, of course. Sallie started dating another guy and eventually married him. Sid, less interested in a platonic relationship than Sal was, rode off on his motorcycle. I lost contact.

This story is about breaking some barriers by asking questions, taking risks and seeing others through Christ's eyes. It isn't a "success story"—Sid didn't pray to become a Christian. I wish he had. I wonder who is willing to cross some barriers to get into his life now. Who can share with him about the love of Christ? Maybe someone could pick up where I left off. Maybe you?

I know what you're thinking. You're thinking that would never happen to you. You're thinking, *Yeah, right, what does this have to do with my life?* But that only proves my point that we think about outcasts from a carefully protected, comfortable, academic distance. I thought the same thing. So did the disciples (they probably thought it radical to go grocery shopping in Samaria).

Jesus thinks differently. His stories are filled with talk about those on the outside coming inside to eat with him. He talks about those who were despised and rejected becoming first. He talks about parties and wedding receptions filled with the wrong kind of people.

His actions were just as shocking as his words. He ate with biker-types. In fact he used eating and drinking at the same table (or at the same well) as his tool to break barriers of social ostracism throughout the Gospels.[1]

Jesus has a special place in his heart for the outcast. That's who *he* was. Jesus lived as an outcast. He was despised and rejected and misunderstood and alone. To dismiss the possibility of reaching those who are social outcasts is to risk not knowing Jesus.

Furthermore, when God loves *us* he is reconciling the outcast. We were all, at one time, outcasts—"without hope and without God in the world" (Eph 2:12). So we replicate God's love for us when we reach out to outcasts. To not reach out to the outcast means we slight God's very work in us.

Outcasts Are People Too

So if you meet Sid—or whoever are outcasts for you—remember the story of the woman at the well. Be willing to reach out. Start by asking some questions. It was Jesus' prelude to sharing the gospel. It can be ours too.

Outcasts for some are friends for others. It's helpful to identify outcasts in your life. Look for people you are isolated from because of social barriers. Then when a potential divine appointment arises, you'll be more likely to take advantage of it.

Here are some helpful steps to help us cross some barriers—even if the outcast is the person next door.

1. Tell others you are interested in their life. If you can't do that, do what I did with Sid: tell others to tell others you're interested in their life. Don't be afraid to ask. There are nice people who wear leather and have tattoos.

2. Cross social hurdles by asking questions. Investigate their lives. How else was I going to learn about a chopped bike or what it was like to have a pet wolf? (Yes, a real, live pet wolf.) Get to know them.

3. Ask them to help you do something you can't do on your own. Jesus asked the woman at the well for a favor—a drink. I asked for a ride on a Harley. I know, motorcycles are dangerous. Live a little, take a risk. It shocked Sid that a Christian was interested in his world, and I don't blame him. It seems we spend so much time at religious functions, potlucks and committee meetings we barely have time for involvement in others' lives.

A friend of mine wanted to start a relationship with a Jewish friend at work. He began by asking his coworker how he dealt with life in a pluralist society. After all, the American Jewish culture has worked at it for hundreds of years; Christians are just starting. Asking for real advice and help in an important area was a great opener.

4. Find out about their pain. Fears, pain, sorrow are all opportunities to share about how Christ will meet us in our need. Cops' "John Wayning" Sid was an open door to go to a deeper level of a relationship.

5. Make a transition to spiritual issues. Remember it's okay to just talk and enjoy a conversation with someone. But if the opportunity comes, be ready to pick up on a spiritual topic or even ask spiritual questions if it's appropriate. If it doesn't happen, that's okay, the Spirit is doing his work at his own speed.

Here are some questions that Paul Little used to make that transition. He would ask someone, "Are you interested in spiritual things?" (Most people will answer in some kind of positive way.)

His next question would be, "What do you think a real Christian is?" (The consistency of response here is amazing: someone active in church, someone who lives a good life, someone who follows the teachings of Christ.)

Then the next comment would follow naturally: "Well, those are certainly things Christians *do,* but they aren't what a real Christian *is.* A real Christian is someone who has a personal relationship with Christ."[2]

Crossing social hurdles with questions does good things for us. It expands *our* world. Who wouldn't like to get out of their holy huddles and do some really interesting stuff? It makes us braver. Once you've shared with people outside your sphere, those inside won't seem quite so intimidating. Besides, a ride on a Harley beats the heck out of a potluck supper.

Questions for Reflection or Discussion
1. What social barriers did Christ cross when he spoke to the Samaritan woman? What consequences do you think he risked?
2. What changes happened to allow Mack to cross barriers with Motorcycle Sid?
3. What social barriers face you? What changes need to happen so you can cross those barriers?

Pray that God will give you the strength to cross barriers with the gospel.

• Nine •

The Power of Positive Evangelism

Positive thinking is attractive to the world. A French clinic during the 1800s made its patients quote this positive message: "Every day in every way I am getting better and better." This was found to aid in recovery.

Since then people have been looking in mirrors and saying positive things. It goes beyond mental and physical healing; marketing management, for example, often requires salespeople to quote positive ditties to themselves: "I'm a salesman and I love it." (Repeat.)

The premise is that lack of faith in ourselves erodes our potential. If you just believe in yourself you can do anything.[1] And it works . . . at least to a point.

The power of positive thinking is not reserved for the secular. It was a minister, Norman Vincent Peale, who popularized the idea of positive thinking in the fifties. His book *The Power of Positive Thinking* sold millions. His teaching had a profound impact on the church and our society. Some claim his book was even the instrument God used to bring them to faith in Christ. Peale states that positive thinking is another way to think of faith. He uses, as his proof text, Paul's words, "I can do all things in him who strengthens me" (Phil 4:13 RSV).[2]

Yet when I meet a disciple of Peale or of others like him, I get an unsettled feeling. As pastor Roy Clements says, "It almost seems that some who follow the power of positive thinking have mistaken faith for self-hypnosis."

Positive thinking seems to mean, "You can do it if you believe hard enough in yourself." But there are things we can't do ourselves, no matter how hard we believe. In college I felt called to be pre-med. I believed in myself. I got 13 out of a possible 100 on my first chemistry exam, but I was a true believer. Undaunted, I sweated out the years as a microbiology major, but I still turned out more *pre* than *med*. Belief in myself was not a factor. (There are worse cases. Take the guy who truly believes he's Caesar Augustus, for instance.)

It seems that those who would follow Peale's advice are encouraged to place their faith in themselves, not God, regardless of the evidence. But believing in ourselves is heresy. The Bible never tells us to believe in anything but God.

Sure, there is a power in being positive. It's hard to look at the life of the apostle Paul without seeing positive action and thought being put into practice. But being positive about something false is dangerous.

Paul was constantly telling people not to be anxious, but in everything to give thanksgiving to God. He told them that from jail—he was no armchair coach. But Paul recognized that positive thinking is only as good as its object. We don't praise God because we condition ourselves to praise him; we praise him because he is trustworthy, faithful and true. That's why, after contrasting the confidence of Paul and Peale, so many have concluded, "I find Paul appealing and Peale appalling."

Unfortunately, but naturally, the power of positive thinking has spilled over into evangelism. It's just too easy to confuse evangelism with marketing.

I want to be the kind of person, like Jesus, who reaches out to people he meets on the road of life. Yet even now I feel a hesitancy inside me when talking to others about spiritual subjects. Part of that is healthy; when we share our faith we are dealing with eternal matters which should carry some weight. Yet there's a hesitancy that comes from a lack of confidence.

True Confidence
So we try to be positive, but in the wrong way. We try to gain confidence by whipping up a psychological event. We look in the mirror and say, "I can do it, I can share, and when I get to heaven I'll see my fruit there." Well, I hope that's true, but not because we've manipulated ourselves into acting confident. Rather, *our confidence comes from our belief in who we are before God and in the message we share.*

That's where Jesus' confidence came from: not from a psychological event he had manufactured but from the certainty of his status as God's Son. There is a power of positive evangelism, but only when we are confident about the right things. Jesus modeled it.

"Jesus answered her, 'If you knew the gift of God and who it is that asks you for a drink, you would have asked him and he would have given you living water' " (Jn 4:10).

These are not the words of an insecure person. Christ's confidence allowed him to approach people not as if he were making an unwanted interruption in their day, but with the power of positive evangelism.

When the woman questioned Jesus, he didn't wither from embarrassment ("Gosh, you're right, I'm not supposed to talk to you, what was I thinking, please forgive me"). No, he continued the conversation with a winsome and bold claim.

Though his response was couched in parable, Jesus claimed he was more important than he might appear. Jesus' confidence sprang from his identity as a child of God. "If you knew who was talking to you . . ." he said. Though thirsty and tired, he claimed to possess a valuable gift from God—and it was hers for the asking.

Jesus could have given a very different response to her. He could have started with a negative critique of her lifestyle and the things she needed to change before she would get the living water. As we'll see in the next chapter, this woman's character had some room for improvement. But he chose to couch his message in a positive light. Positive about what was being offered. Positive about her chance of receiving it. Jesus practiced confident, positive evangelism—and so should we.

Contradiction in Terms?

It seems I've created another paradox, doesn't it? I've said Jesus' humility attracted me. I've said we should follow the model of humility Jesus charts for us. I've said a humble request is better than a power play. Now I say Jesus' *confidence* is a model too. But it's not a contradiction. Confidence is not the opposite of humility; arrogance is. Vulnerability—weakness on purpose—takes tremendous confidence.

C. S. Lewis framed it this way: "When I became a man I put away childish things, including my fear of childishness, and the desire to be very grown up."[3]

It was spring in Kentucky. Time for basketball tournaments and horse racing and our annual outreach week at the University of Kentucky.

During the day we hosted forums, booktables and student outreach parties. Staff and students even came from colleges in Ohio to help us. After one of the outreach events Allen, a new I-V staffworker in Ohio, approached me.

"Umm, Mack," he said hesitantly, "you know lots about evangelism, and, well, I haven't really ever gone up to someone and just talked to them about the faith."

I realized this was a confession.

"Would you mind taking me to do evangelism?" he blurted out.

I didn't feel like explaining that he needn't feel guilty about not being an expert on evangelism (being on staff doesn't make someone an expert). I didn't have time to tell him I felt the same way when I first came on staff (the difference was, I *pretended* to be an expert). I left the part about "doing evangelism" alone. I just said "Sure." And then I pointed to some rainbow people sitting in the grassy quad by the library and said, "Let's talk to them." I started walking.

Allen sucked air in through his clenched teeth. He tried to make his case as we walked—"Well, I thought we might first spend some time . . ." But it was too late. In a few short steps we were hovering over the small group.

"Hi," I said. The group looked up. Two guys and a woman. They lowered their cigarettes.

"My name's Mack and this is Allen." Allen's mouth was open. His index finger was still raised to the sky in mid-punctuation. As I said his name, he raised a couple more fingers to match his index finger and wiggled them all in a weak greeting. The rainbow folk said, "Hi, Allen." Allen closed his mouth.

Rainbow people are hippie "wannabes." Long hair, tie-dyed

shirts, beads, marijuana leaf jewelry. I felt nostalgic.

"Allen and I are doing something crazy," I started. They smiled at Allen. He looked as if he agreed. "We're with this Christian group called InterVarsity," I continued, "and we've sponsored a week of activity to get people to think about the claims of Christ. We were wondering if we could ask you guys about what you think about Jesus."

They looked at each other.

"We're not pushing anything on anyone, we really just what to know what you think," I added.

"Well, sure," one of them said. "In fact, we saw the banner and were wondering what was going on over there."

After they introduced themselves I said, "That banner's a good place to start. When you see a poster or banner about something Christian, what's your first impression?"

The discussion was off and running. We asked questions. They asked questions. It was fun. I remember we talked about "It-doesn't-matter-what-we-believe-just-as-long-as-we're-sincere." (I usually ask questions about Adolf Hitler's sincerity in these discussions. This time was no exception.)

The woman smiled a sweet smile, as if she was letting me in on a secret, and said, "You know, bottom line, Christianity just isn't true for me." (This has become an unchallenged campus mantra.)

"How do you *know* it's not true for you?" I asked. The smile left her face. She studied the tree behind me. Clearly no one had asked her this before.

I continued, "Many people have made decisions about Christ without looking at what he says. You might be surprised—he just might be truth for you."

After a minute Allen jumped in. He was paraphrasing C. S. Lewis: "If Jesus was who he claimed, he didn't leave open the possibility that . . ." It was a great point, and one of the rainbow folk was nodding his head. It was such a good point I realized Allen would do just fine without me. He just needed a bit of confidence and that was all.

"I have to go," I said. "These guys are all yours." The rainbow folk said, "Bye, Mack." I knew I wasn't leaving Allen outnumbered: God always makes a majority.

Perhaps, like Allen, you want to be able to talk to people you meet along your journey and "give away your faith." Yet you also feel his hesitation. You don't want to blow it by saying something stupid. Perhaps you have a hard time knowing how to bring up the subject. Maybe you're afraid others will lump you in with the evangelistic oddballs out there (there are lots of those). Perhaps you fear that you're going to have to spin intellectual cartwheels explaining the difference between canonical and apocryphal Scripture. You might even feel that if someone came up to you and told you they wanted to become a Christian, you'd totally forget the gospel outline you've dutifully memorized. Perhaps you notice confidence always seems to elude you just when you need it most.

Don't despair. My confidence for our discussion didn't come easy—it came through some difficult and awkward learning moments, and not all of them were evangelistic moments. I can be a positive evangelist today not because I've hypnotized myself in front of a mirror, but because I came to believe what the Bible says about me is true.

Do You Know Yourself?

Because evangelism is a difficult and forced activity without a strong understanding of our identity in God, I often start our training for missions and evangelism with a session on self-image. Usually people think this an odd start. After all, they came to hear about how to share their faith, not about their self-image. But the connection works like this: When my identity is rooted in the truth of Scripture about myself as God's child, I can see I really have something valuable to offer others—regardless of the response or of how I feel. When my identity is not rooted in the truth of Scripture, I apologize for being alive. This truth didn't sink into me till I had been teaching it for some time. (Some say the eighteen-inch journey from our heads to our hearts is the longest journey of all.)

Leeann and I teach a program designed to equip students for crosscultural ministry. We start the program with various trust exercises, and we talk about a Christian self-image. Easy to teach, hard to know. The first year, I taught the session poorly—no surprise since I had not internalized the very thing I was trying to teach. I felt the bad session reflected poorly on me. A big fight with Leeann developed, destroying what confidence she had. The embarrassment of the session paled when I realized I had acted in the very way I told the students not to. I just couldn't believe I was still valuable when I failed.

After some soul-searching (and an apology to Leeann), I realized the need to internalize what I wanted to teach. I took a hard look at myself. It came as no surprise to those around me when I discovered I was far too worried about what people thought of me. All my friends know I'm a people pleaser, and part of that is fine; it's who God has made me. The problem becomes insidious when I try to gain my identity from those around me rather than from Christ.

Where does your identity come from? Beware. The world offers a plethora of ways to gain an identity through avenues other than Christ. The world would have us believe our identity is no bigger than being born to shop. The world's view says we're random bits of protoplasm. The world says we're just dysfunctional sons and daughters of dysfunctional parents. The world says, "With a good mirror and a positive ditty you can own the world."

But God says he forgives us. God credits Christ's righteousness to our account. God says he has adopted us as his children and is making us whole. He says our identity stems from the fact we are sons and daughters of a loving, healing heavenly Father. He says he chose us in love for a glorious future. He says his love is so strong he can't stop loving us, no matter what.

God even says his love for us is so complete and perfect that *there is nothing we can do to make him love us more.* He won't love us more if we attend every church function; he won't love us more if we witness to everyone we meet; he won't love us more if we become missionaries in Mombasa (you wouldn't believe how many people think God will love them more if they move to Mombasa).

Understand, I'm not offering a cure-all for brokenness. It can take years to work through brokenness and pain in our lives. But developing our identity as God's children lays a groundwork for becoming a confident witness. To accept what *God* says is true about us forms our identity as God's children. It then becomes foundational for evangelism. After all, we can't tell others the good news if we think, *The good news applies to everybody but me.*

Paul said it like this: "Such confidence as this [to minister the gospel] is ours through Christ before God. Not that we are competent in ourselves to claim anything for ourselves, but our competence comes from God" (2 Cor 3:4-5).

We are competent to minister, not out of our own strength, not because we believe in ourselves, but because we are now sons and daughters of God. This confidence in our Christian identity allows us to reach out to people around us and turn regular encounters into divine appointments. That's the power of positive evangelism.

Questions for Reflection or Discussion

1. Reread 2 Corinthians 3:4-6. Where does Paul say our confidence is from?

2. What things erode your evangelistic confidence? How might you be tempted to gain confidence apart from Christ?

3. How does a biblical self-image help us share our faith?

Pray that Paul's words in 2 Corinthians 3:4-6 will make that long, eighteen-inch journey from your head to your heart, and pray that God will guard you from false methods of confidence.

Ten

The Hooker
at the Well

Pete and I overloaded our plates from the breakfast bar at Shoney's. Pete was new in town. He moved from Washington, D.C., to Lexington, Kentucky, after finishing his political appointment. The shift was a career change from politics to sales. We spent breakfast getting reacquainted, having known each other in Tennessee.

I asked Pete if there had been any difficulties in the transition. Pete told me about the house not selling back in D.C., he told me about the hunt for a new church . . . and there was something else. He shifted uncomfortably in his seat and contemplated his last half-eaten donut.

"Something happened that I was completely unprepared for at work," Pete said, shaking his head.

"What?" I asked.

"I mean, this is something that's never happened to me."

I swallowed. Pete glanced up at me, then looked back at the table and said, "Well, I went into our training time with the thought that I was really going to reach out to the people I work with, so during our training week in Atlanta I'd go out with the group rather than just go back to the hotel room."

I nodded.

"Well, there's this woman. She's older—divorced—and she started hitting on me." Pete looked up and searched my face.

"And?" I said.

"Well, she was hitting on me hard. Like, you know, grabbing my knee under the table, and putting her arm around me."

"What did you do?"

"I didn't know what to do. I pulled out the pictures of the kids from my wallet. I started telling her how happy I was to be married. I said what a good churchgoer I was and all." Pete looked sheepish; I exhaled.

Pete smiled at the server as he gave us our check.

Then he said, "I guess I felt bad that I didn't do better telling her about my faith. I don't want to look like a nerd, but how do you tell someone about the gospel when they're coming on to you? Maybe I shouldn't be so hard on myself, but I just didn't know how to respond in a relevant way."

It's a Crazy World

Pete voiced a concern many of us feel. How *do* we get our message out to a world which seems wildly out of sync with the message of Christ?

"Sir," the woman said, "you have nothing to draw with and the well is deep. Where can you get this living water? Are you greater than our father Jacob, who gave us the well and drank from it himself, as did also his sons and his flocks and herds?"

Jesus answered, "Everyone who drinks this water will be thirsty again, but whoever drinks the water I give him will never thirst. Indeed, the water I give him will become in him a spring of water welling up to eternal life."

The woman said to him, "Sir, give me this water so that I won't get thirsty and have to keep coming here to draw water."

He told her, "Go, call your husband and come back."

"I have no husband," she replied.

Jesus said to her, "You are right when you say you have no husband. The fact is, you have had five husbands, and the man you now have is not your husband. What you have just said is quite true." (Jn 4:11-18)

The dynamics of this subtle but relevant passage often elude us. The conversation is shocking beyond the ethnic taboos of the day. Upright men did not speak to unknown women in public. This was forbidden. To modern ears it may seem like an ordinary request for water, but in Jesus' day it was as if he asked, "Have you got a boyfriend?" rather than "Will you give me a drink?" Conversation across gender lines during Jesus' day (and to this day in many parts of the world) was thought to express a desire for a sexual relationship.

It's even more shocking considering who she was. Her lifestyle brought revulsion from the community. It would be generous to call her promiscuous; she would win no awards for her family values.

Her looks, though, might have won awards. The text doesn't call her attractive, but she was. She had enchanted five men despite her past. Probably married at age thirteen, she reached the legal divorce limit three husbands later.[1] Marrying the fourth man sealed her reputation as an easy woman. After the fifth divorce she no longer cared: she now lived with a guy she hadn't bothered to marry.

Why trouble myself? she probably thought. *It won't last.*

Her promiscuity had become a lifestyle—a lifestyle that didn't stop when she met a man at the well. Speaking to Jesus was a signal—as clear as the winking of the woman at Broadway and Main wearing fishnet hose.

Biblical scholars agree that the woman at the well avoided the ostracism of the other women in her village by drawing water at noon, rather than in the cool of the day.[2] But she could draw water from two wells: the one in the village or Jacob's well at the fork of the road outside town (they are both still there).[3] If she wanted to avoid ostracism by drawing water at noon, she could have avoided ostracism closer to her door. Why did she go to Jacob's well?

Africans read this passage with more insight. After all, they know more about public wells. They see a woman who is looking for something other than water. They see a woman visiting the watering hole at the time and place men stopped their travels. This woman wasn't looking for water. She was looking for sex.[4]

And if she misinterpreted Jesus' intentions she had her reasons:

If he's breaking rules by talking to me, what other rules does he want to break?

Does he really possess God's gift? I've been lied to by men before.

If this water is for free, then he's the first man to offer me something with no strings attached.

Oh well, any excitement to escape this drudgery . . . besides, he's got a kind face . . .

We may miss these dynamics, but Jesus doesn't. When he says "call your husband," he is not being sexist. Jesus often talked to women, even hookers. No, Jesus listens to her. And he tells her to stop flirting with him. He's offering something better than sex.

This passage explodes with new meaning if this woman is

"hitting on" Jesus. To understand the difference, don't read this passage monotone; read it with a breathy "I have no husband." Add to it her seductive smile and half-opened eyes. It's not what she says to Jesus, it's what she is thinking.

Her half-lie, "I have no husband," is a way to say, "I'm available to you."[5] With those words she offers herself to one more man, betraying the man she is living with.

But it was her last betrayal. Jesus wasn't just one more man.

Listen to the World

Jesus saw beneath the words and actions to her real longings. He knew her brokenness; he understood her need. He knew those things better than she did, because he listened—really listened.

John Stott was asked to speak at a conference on "What should the church say to the world?" Graciously he reminded the conference planners that the prior question should be, "How can we listen to the world before we speak?"[6]

Stott suggests three questions he hears around the globe. Though they are expressed in different ways, their roots remain the same:

1. What does my life mean?
2. How can I find a spiritual reality?
3. Where can I find love?

Here's a simple hearing test: In what specific ways are the people around me seeking meaning, spiritual reality and love?

Since the list of substitutes for love, meaning and God is endless, Christians (those who listen) will hear these questions all around us. The substitutes are endlessly unsatisfying too: eating and exercise, beer, affairs, money, sports, cars, cults, shopping, jobs, success. We don't need to major in psychology to see it's true—we just need to listen.

Pete commented, "It's a new idea to me that my coworker was searching for love or meaning, not sex, but it makes sense."

Translate the Scriptures

Jesus didn't only listen; he had answers. And when he answered he didn't speak in his heavenly language. He didn't speak in academic Greek. He didn't use metaphors with lost meanings—no "washed-in-the-blood" talk. When Jesus spoke he used the colloquial language of the day and employed illustrations that had meaning to the listener.[7]

Look how his words spoke to the woman at the well. Deep within she longed for something—anything—to splash over herself and cleanse away the filth she felt in life. The most she could do, by herself, was another empty marriage or the rush of a one-night stand. But it was like salty water—it only added to her thirst.

When Jesus spoke to her about living water welling up to eternity, it hit her right where she lived. To hear Jesus talk you'd think she was *worth* something! How long had it been since anyone implied she had real worth? He said life eternal was hers for the asking. Jesus offered meaning and spiritual reality in her own language.

We need to speak like that. We need answers for the heartfelt questions in the language of the day. This combination of listening to the world and translating the scriptural truth is a working definition of Christian relevance. And like any translation project, it takes thoughtful work.

I was at a skiing and mountain-climbing school in Zermatt, Switzerland. It was before I became a Christian. I remember asking my friend Robert, "Why do you go to parties with all of us but don't drink?" It was a genuine question, and his genuine answer is the reason I pursued Christ. He said, "Mack, it's not that I don't sometimes want to. It's just that I know what I have inside me is so much better than what I could get out of a bottle."

His one sentence was a bit of outstanding translation work. Without my knowing it, he translated a hint of the gospel in a way that neither sacrificed its truth nor deadened its appeal. It was in my language. He spoke of something better—it had the hint of spirituality and meaning. He didn't condemn me or my friends. And his hint sparked interest in me. It invited response without leaving me feeling bludgeoned.

Later, I searched him out and told him I wanted what he had. We were in a small hotel room. I remember the noise from the dance band rumbling through that room—the room where I told Christ I would follow him. Perhaps that's why I want Pete to know how to share his faith when he finds himself in a similar hotel bar today.

How to Respond to Misunderstandings

Look how Jesus deals with the woman's misunderstandings. She mistakes Jesus' words as meaning physical water. She mistakes Jesus' intentions as sexual. But Jesus is ready. Jesus avoids two pitfalls. He is neither shocked by the woman's lifestyle nor attracted by her advances.

Shock often elicits "righteous responses"—an angry rebuke, an evangelistic monologue. But Jesus doesn't assume a holy posture, furrowing his brows and calling her a woman of ill repute.

Jesus avoids the opposite extreme, too: mistaking her words as genuine interest in him. He doesn't straighten his tie suddenly, thinking of how attractive he is. Jesus has done his homework about the world around him. So when she tries to pick him up he knows what it means and how to respond.

What he does do is tell her to get her husband. This is

unexpected integrity from a man willing to break other social codes. Jesus' directive to get her husband and come back tells the woman he wants to continue talking, but not for the reasons she thinks. It says he is interested in her, not sex.

Misunderstandings will happen to us, too. It's as sure as rain. Scripture tells us that the world is blinded to spiritual reality. And what reason could folks have to think differently if they don't know the love of Christ? If we are involved in the world we need to plan for misunderstandings. Responding with integrity to misunderstandings is the pattern of Jesus.

Misunderstandings don't mean the opportunity is over. Jesus used the woman's misunderstanding as a bigger opportunity. So don't be put off; defensiveness is a killer to any conversation—especially a religious one.

Don't become blinded by the world, either, and forget the truth we proclaim. Some shouldn't be in a hotel bar at all, if it's a place of temptation for them. There is a time to run from dangerous temptations.

Do be ready to explain why Christ is worth a life of integrity. Do respond in a way that says you are interested in a person, no matter how you feel about what they are doing or how badly they've misunderstood your intentions.

When Pete tried to reach out to his coworkers, he went to the hotel bar saying, "I'm going to be involved in your world. I'm coming on your terms, just as Jesus came to us all." But that's not what his coworkers thought.

Pete's coworkers had mistaken Pete's cue. What they thought was, "Pete's here to make business contacts or to get drunk or for sex—just like everyone else."

In one sense Pete is right: he shouldn't be so hard on himself. His integrity, as awkward as it was, may have been as important as any word, even if all he did was share with the bold woman that he was a goody-two-shoes. As Nigel Lee says, "We mustn't become so much like the unbelievers that they have no questions to ask us." It occurred to Pete only later that God was honoring his intention to share his faith (isn't it amazing how often God rudely interrupts our evangelistic efforts with opportunities to share our faith?).

Next time, Pete said, he would be ready with a modern-day equivalent of "Go get your husband and come back." Today, to some, it's radical to say, "I don't go to bed with someone I haven't made a lifelong commitment to. What I've got helps me really love people."

Listen to the Spirit

It shouldn't surprise us that Jesus knows more of the woman's life than what she told him: Jesus listened to the Spirit. Jesus' ironic observation, "What you have said is quite true: you've had five husbands," comes from the Spirit's voice. And his insight brings her flirtation to a halt.

Perhaps you're thinking, "Yeah, but he was God and I am not." Yes, he was fully God, but he laid his omniscience aside to be like us. He relied on the Holy Spirit just as we do. When Jesus said "you've had five husbands," he was operating on inside information from the Spirit.

I wish I could blow someone away with inside information during an evangelistic conversation. (That's probably why it has never happened to me.) I'd love to blurt out, "Oh, by the way, God told me that Joe just broke up with you and you're thinking of moving in with Gene just to get back at Joe." But that has not been my experience.

With me it's usually more ordinary, like what happened when my sister accepted Christ. I saw no visions, but I was aware that the Spirit was at work. There was a feeling that I stood on holy ground; the Spirit alerted me to his work.

Here's how I listen for the Spirit in conversations and relationships.

Who is God bringing into my life? Are some of these people ones who don't know Christ? Is there someone who seems to be open to spiritual conversation? Lord, are you setting me up?

What conversations about spiritual issues seem to click? Have I answered some question that has been on someone's mind about faith?

When I think about sharing my faith, does someone come to mind?

I realize these are not very flashy listenings. That's okay. A vast amount of kingdom building happens in the ordinary.

At other times, unknown to me, the Spirit will lead me to an idea or even a word that is somehow important for a person's conversion.

Focusing on the dramatic, though, means we miss the bigger picture. It's the Holy Spirit who empowers *all* parts of spiritual encounters. The Holy Spirit leads Jesus to Samaria for a divine encounter. The Holy Spirit gives Jesus strength for humility. The Holy Spirit gives Jesus the ears to listen to the world around him. The Holy Spirit gives power to translate truth into words with meaning in the day-to-day world. The Holy Spirit gives power to live a life of integrity in a world out of sync. And sometimes —sometimes—the Holy Spirit gives insights that seem like inside information.

The reason many feel powerless in evangelism today is that we're hooked on techniques rather than filled with the Spirit. Make sure, when you are engaging your world with the good news of Christ, to listen to the Holy Spirit in every way, not just the dramatic. The power of Jesus for evangelism came through the Holy Spirit. It does for us too.

Pete and I agreed that relevance is more than buying the right clothes and watching colleagues swill beers. Relevance is learning how to speak timeless truth to a world in flux through the power of the Holy Spirit. That's the relevance of Christ.

Questions for Reflection or Discussion
1. According to John Stott, what are the questions all around us?
2. How do you see those questions reflected in the woman at the well? In Pete's coworker in the hotel bar?
3. When Jesus responded to the woman at the well, how did he speak in her language? How did he model integrity? How did he listen to the Spirit?

Pray that you will become a better listener to the world, the Word and the Spirit.

• Eleven •

Questions

Charley really doesn't like Sara very much. But one day it hits him: *The way to help Sara is to date her! If we were to go out, my strengths could rub off on her and she would be far better off for it. It will require sacrifice on my part, but it's the least I can do.*

So Charley marches up to Sara's door with a book entitled *100 Things Sara Needs to Change in Order to Become a Real Person.* He rings the doorbell. When she answers, he shoves the book in her face and states, "I've decided it would be best for you if we date. When you finish reading this, I'll be waiting in my truck."

Charley is Gene Breitenbach's description of modern-day evangelism in America.[1] It's sad but true. Sad because evangelism in America often resembles a bad date. Charley may know some important apologetics, but since he hasn't approached Sara in an attractive way, the important things won't translate. Charley and Sara aren't going to get engaged anytime soon.

The Dangers of Apologetics

Apologetics (the branch of theology concerned with the defense or proof of the gospel) can do dangerous things. Without simple principles guiding our answers, we can do more harm than good as we try to defend the gospel.

For one thing, sticking people with the right answers won't guarantee they'll turn to Christ. In fact, the smug answer, however correct, may ensure that a non-Christian will never listen to a Christian again. Christianity is not information transfer. Christianity is a relationship.

Anyone married for more than six weeks understands this. The real issue in a disagreement with a spouse is not how logical, how accurate or how right either spouse is, but how they treat one another.

Apologetics is dangerous for another reason. I meet many Christians with a deep personal relationship with Christ who are insecure about evangelism. They feel they can't share their faith if they lack a comprehensive answer for every possible question. They mistakenly think their lack of an answer will prevent someone from turning to Christ. Yet new Christians—the ones with the least knowledge of their faith—are often the ones who are most effective at sharing their faith. People's real questions, the ones deep in their hearts, are usually met through other avenues: compassion, integrity, humor.

Finally, apologetics can work to mask the real issues a person is facing. Academic questions often become smoke screens keeping Christ at arm's length. Most discussions I've had about the Spanish Inquisition have had more to do with psychology than theology. We should guard ourselves from being sidetracked from a real issue because we have a right answer to a nonissue.

Two Christian students were talking with a woman they had just met on campus. They began a discussion about Christianity. She asked them about the problem of evil, then hypocrites in the church. Evolution topped off the discussion. The two Christian students felt undone with each question, saying that they understood why this was a problem but they really didn't have much in the way of an answer. Yet at the end of the discussion they asked the woman if she would like to accept Christ. "Yes," she said, "I see genuine hope in what you guys are offering."

We offer real hope in Christ. As it turned out, for this young woman hope was more important than answers.

In Defense of Apologetics

So should we dump apologetics? By no means. Let me give you three reasons:

1. Remember, apologetics is not apologies. When we decide to follow Christ, we set a course in life. *Anyone who decides to live a certain lifestyle is called on from time to time to explain why.* So we must be able to defend our choice and our actions. This is not so much a function of being Christian as of just being human.[2]

2. Answering questions doesn't make people Christians, but *unanswered questions can prevent people from becoming Christians.*[3] Yes, it's true that no one has ever been argued into the kingdom, but it's also true that no one has ever become a Christian without some reason.[4]

3. *Jesus made his case through a reasoned defense,* so we should be ready to do the same.[5] (This is perhaps the most important reason.)

So how do we resolve this tension between the danger of apologetics and the need to defend our faith? It is not an issue

---

122

of learning better and better apologetics. The real issue facing Christians today is knowing *how to use* apologetics.

"Sir," the woman said, "I can see that you are a prophet. Our fathers worshiped on this mountain, but you Jews claim that the place where we must worship is in Jerusalem."

Jesus declared, "Believe me, woman, a time is coming when you will worship the Father neither on this mountain nor in Jerusalem. You Samaritans worship what you do not know; we worship what we do know, for salvation is from the Jews. Yet a time is coming and has now come when the true worshipers will worship the Father in spirit and truth, for they are the kind of worshipers the Father seeks. God is spirit, and his worshipers must worship in spirit and in truth."

The woman said, "I know that Messiah" (called Christ) "is coming. When he comes, he will explain everything to us."

Then Jesus declared, "I who speak to you am he." (Jn 4:19-26)

To say Jesus makes the woman at the well uncomfortable is an understatement. Jesus jars her from her sexy come-on to the stark realization that they are talking about different things. Once her ugly life is exposed, she does the sensible thing: she changes the subject. Who wouldn't?

She makes the switch from her sex life to religion in a clever way. The question of worship for the Samaritans was the religious hot potato of the day. It's as if she said, "Umm, well, ah . . . what do you think about abortion?" or "By the way, is Christianity the only way to God?" or "How can a good God allow evil?" Any issue to move the attention off her. This discussion is a smoke screen. It's her attempt to mask the naked feeling that comes from knowing she is talking with someone who knows everything—a frightening thought.

Consider the Context

Her question is ironic, considering who he is. Jesus is the one sent to restore proper worship with God. If she had bowed down and worshiped him right then, she would have worshiped at the right place. And Jesus would have been within his rights to demand this of her. But Jesus was sensitive to the situation. He was sensitive to the person. His response to her questions had heart.

The context, in this case, is a question from an embarrassed and uneducated prostitute in Samaria. Jesus would prove much sharper with people who should know more, but in this case he doesn't skewer her with a sarcastic reply, he doesn't turn his nose up at her (as many did, no doubt), he doesn't even remind her that she is changing the subject. He takes her question seriously because he takes *her* seriously. We think of this woman with respect today because Jesus treated her that way.

We too are to take people seriously. We remember that our job is not to outwit people but to win hearts. Our responses need heart. How do we avoid the smug response?

We need to ask what the questioner means when he or she asks a question. In the last chapter we noted there is a triple listening: to the world, the Word and the Spirit. This gives us a platform to speak in a relevant way. The next step is to understand the context of specific questions. Different people may ask the same question but get different answers because of the context.

Remember there are more important things than having the right answer. As the old saying goes, "People want to know we care before they care what we know."

I remember speaking with a freshman named Justin in the student center at the University of Tennessee. It looked like every other student center: plastic chairs, dirty floor, noisy MTV flickering in the background. Justin's backpack was draped over one chair while he was draped over another. He told me, proudly, that he was taking an honors English class and going into theater. He wanted to air his objections about Christianity to me. I was eating a rubbery hamburger and listening.

"I mean," he said in an airy way, "how could God let bad things happen to people? Look, if God is all-powerful, and if God is good, and if evil exists . . ." His eyes were intent. It was as if he had just thought this up himself. His right hand slapped his left with each point of the old saw.

Suddenly I'm with him in body only. As he speaks, my mind takes up a memory. It's as if someone has turned the MTV into the noise of a busy emergency room.

In my mind's eye it's as clear as if I'm there. The aseptic smells, the bustle, the pit-of-the-stomach feel. I'm standing over the gurney. The medical lights cast stark shadows. A beautiful young woman lies there in pain. She doesn't scream—she moans. Every time the doctor moves her to suture the gash on her side, her face contorts. But it's not the gash that hurts, it's her broken hips . . . and something else greater than physical pain.

I knew her story from the social worker on the case. He had briefed me, rapid-fire, as we marched down the grim, fluorescent corridor. "They abducted her. They raped her—four or five guys—in the back of their van. They threw her from the van after they finished."

He stopped me as I got ready to go through the double steel doors into the emergency room. "Mack," he said, looking up from his clipboard, "they didn't bother to stop the van."

I see her hand in mine. Her dark brown skin against my white skin. She holds my hand tight. I had planned to ask her some questions, but it seems suddenly worthless. I feel shameful about my masculinity. But there are no women chaplains on call for the emergency room that night. I feel angry. *Where is justice, Lord?* I ask.

I also feel pitifully inadequate. I've been called to answer the "religious question" she's asked everyone—doctors, nurses, police, ambulance folk—people normally numbed to pain, but feeling skittery around her. She's asked them one question over and over. They have no answers, only procedures. *Do I have answers?* I wonder. My throat feels tight.

She looks at my chest and sees my red badge with a yellow cross. "Chaplain Stiles" it says below the cross. Her eyes meet mine. She repeats her question. "Why did God let this happen to me?"

I stare back. I feel frightfully empty. I'm asking a crescendo of questions myself: *God, you can't let me say nothing. God, why did you let this happen to her? God, where are you?* The last question is a panicky scream inside me.

Do you see the difference? Two people ask the same question: Justin, whose greatest struggle with the problem of evil has been his bad case of acne, and a woman brutalized by a gang rape. They are very different questions because of the contexts. If I had stood in that emergency room and launched into an explanation of free will and love-only-being-genuine-if-we-were-given-a-choice, it would have been worse than poor taste or a bad response—it would have been evil.

In the student center Justin drones on about eyes for eyes and teeth for teeth. The hamburger has lost what little appeal it had. I put it down on the plate. I'm still thinking back to the John Gaston Hospital emergency room in Memphis—haunted by that young woman. I remember it was only through God's grace that I had an answer at all.

I see myself leaning over so I'm closer to her ear. She's flat on the table, but she's got both hands around mine now. She's weeping. I whisper to her, "Can you hear me?" She nods. I say my name, I call her by hers. I say, "I'm so sorry."

She asks the question again. I don't know what else to say. And then in a flash I realize that's right: I don't know.

"I don't know why God let this happen to you. But I know evil men took Jesus—they did shameful things to him. And when they were finished they nailed him naked to a cross. He died there alone and in pain. I don't know why this happened to you, but I do know that Christ knows your pain. He weeps with you, he hurts with every ache—he's been through it, and he can walk with you through this."

She squeezes my hand. Hope replaces the crazed look in her eyes. She nods. She says, "Thank you . . . thank you." The orderlies have come to take her. The doctor gives another injection. It starts to take effect. Her hand relaxes, but I hold on until the orderlies wheel her into pre-op.

In the student center I shake my head as if to wake up. Justin is now talking about marginal glosses written by monks in the Middle Ages. *Where do first-year students learn these things?* I wonder. "Justin," I interrupt, "I want to get back to the first objection you raised a little while ago, about the problem of evil. I've had to work through that issue myself. Let me tell you about something that happened to me in an emergency room."

Questions are governed by context. Be sensitive. Apologetics is not like a Coke machine—we don't push a button and get a certain answer. Giving facts is important. But, unfortunately, much of modern apologetics begins and ends with raw facts.

Ask yourself before you answer a question, *Is this person angry? Threatened? Wanting off the hook, or a true seeker?* Ask, too, *If this question is answered will it knock down a true hindrance to faith?* The person may just want to change the subject—or may desperately need a real answer.

Our prayer should be that, whatever the motives behind a person's question, God will guard us from aseptic procedures in apologetics and give us his heart as we offer an answer.

Questions for Reflection or Discussion
1. Define apologetics.
2. List three ways apologetics is dangerous. List three ways it is necessary. How does context resolve this tension?
3. If the woman's question about worship had come from a learned religious professional (like Nicodemus in the previous chapter of John), how might Jesus have answered it differently? Why?

Pray that God will give you wisdom to see the different contexts of questions that come your way.

• Twelve •

Answers

Notice how Jesus answers the woman's questions at the well. He is sensitive not only to the *context* but also to the *content* of each question. And Jesus makes sure that she sees what's important about their discussion: him.

When Jesus gives answers to the woman's question on worship, he is knocking down hindrances in her mind. Notice he does not patronize her: "I'm afraid you just couldn't understand, little lady." No, he shoots straight. She has asked a tough question—she gets a tough answer. He is direct, but only because his answer takes her question seriously. Jesus states facts; he corrects wrong information. Though the question is a potential land mine, Jesus is not thrown off. He doesn't hem and haw: "Gee, I really haven't thought much about where we're supposed to worship." Jesus has done his homework. He knows the history of the problem; he states the critical issue; he has an answer. He even expands the question. Jesus remembers not just context but also content. Though he is sensitive to the heart, he also answers the mind.

So should we. We need to understand what images people have in their heads when we talk to them. And then we need to think through those images with a gospel worldview. By that I don't mean we need to don tweed coats and become biblical scholars—I'm just saying we need to so *live in* the gospel message that it's a part of our life and influences whatever we say or do.

My friend Suzy had this conversation with Todd at a party.

Todd: Yeah, I'm very much a liberal, both political and religious.

Suzy: Oh? What does that mean for you?

Todd: Well, I believe in God and all, but I just don't take the Bible literally all the time.

Suzy: So, do you use the Bible as an authority in your life?

Todd: Yes, in a way, but I don't necessarily believe everything the Bible says.

Suzy: What would you say is your ultimate authority in life?

Todd: Myself, I guess. I read the Bible sometimes, along with the Koran and other scriptures, and I come to my own conclusions about what's true and what's not. I believe that God speaks to individuals about what is true for them.

Suzy: You know, it makes sense to me that some people use the Bible as the ultimate authority in their lives, since it's been considered a revelation from God for thousands of years. I can understand why someone would see it as valid . . . I'm curious, though, why do you see *yourself* as a valid authority?

Suzy told me Todd had a tough time answering this question.

Notice Suzy only asks questions—there are no declarative sentences. She has a grasp of the content (a sure-fire way to see if you understand the issues is to be able to ask good questions).

She remembers the context: she is dealing with a sensitive young male ego. She does not skewer his arrogance (a rather tempting target). Her goal is not to win an argument but to win a heart.

Jesus Keeps His Eye on the Goal

The facts Jesus gives to the woman at the well are almost a passing comment, because he recognizes the need behind her question. He sees that she has shifted the conversation from self to religion. He knows a logical answer is not what she needs; he's going for something bigger.

When Jesus gives answers he does not forget the goal. When Jesus says, "The time is coming when you will worship God in neither place," he is saying that there is a bigger issue at stake than the form of our worship.

Jesus wasn't trying to clear up problems about the place of worship. He wasn't walking her through the mistakes made by her Samaritan forefathers. He pointed her to the bigger issue: she was talking to the Messiah.

Often, when we are talking with someone about the gospel, the conversation touches an area of life that goes too deep: some issue of transcendence, meaning or love. The next thing we know they have changed the subject, just like the woman at the well. Suddenly we're talking about evolution, predestination or sex before marriage.

We can stay on track when we remember, along with Jesus, that there are bigger issues. We need to say, "Something bigger is coming than abortion, the Crusades or hypocrisy: Jesus." Here's an example.

My friend Philip Kishoyian is a Kenyan educator and evangelist. His work with World Vision and other ministries has taken him the length and breadth of Kenya. One day Philip was talking to a young African Marxist and the conversation went like this:

Marxist: (with venom) So you believe in Jesus? He's just a white man's God.

Philip: Oh, no, Jesus was far more African.

Marxist: (defiantly) How?

Philip: Well, Jesus never went to the West, but he came here.

Marxist: Oh?

Philip: Yes, as a child his life was threatened by the authorities. He fled with his family to Africa to avoid persecution. He lived in Africa for years. Jesus was a refugee in Africa.

Philip's discussion opened the mind of this young Marxist. Philip shared important facts; he also recognized that this young Marxist needed to see Jesus in a different light. He needed to see Jesus as someone who could have a bearing on his world. Rather than slamming misguided Christians who used Jesus for personal gain, Philip stuck to the facts about Christ. We are not called to defend the wrong things that Christians have done in the past; we are called to get people to think about Jesus.

Putting It Together
Conversations come with no guarantee; they are live things, not static like a book. But here is a pattern I've found helpful to touch people's hearts and minds and reveal the Messiah:

1. *Understand where the question comes from.* This may involve some study on your part.

2. *Affirm a good question.* Credibility goes up when you show some understanding of why a person might ask a certain question.

3. As you give a real answer, *work to reveal Jesus.* Don't get sidetracked from what's important.

Here's a conversation I had a couple of months ago that illustrates the point.

"You don't *really* believe in hell, do you?" Tracy's question

came with the inflection, "You don't *seem* like an ax murderer."
Why does this question always come first? I wondered to myself.
Why doesn't someone ask me what I think about Habitat for Humanity, or what heaven will be like, or whether I admire Mother Teresa?

I took a breath. "Well, Tracy, I know it's very unpopular to believe in hell, and in some ways hell may seem unfair. You need to understand this is a hard thing—Christians struggle with this too. At root the question is 'Is this God you believe in a good God?' "

Tracy said, "Yes." She looked surprised that I understood the problem.

"I know you believe in justice. You're a lawyer." (I know, this doesn't always follow logically, but she *is* a legal activist working for the poor in Lexington.) She nodded.

"Well, it's because of justice that there's a hell. There's a hell for the same reason there are prisons. Look," I said, waving my hands in the air, "let's get rid of the images from Dante's inferno—torture, prisons and burning rocks. Hell's worse than that, but those images don't tell us the *whys*.

"Hell is the final separation from all that's good. Christians believe that anything good comes from God—joy, love, health, goodness, nature, beauty—all these things were created by God.

"But the Bible says we are in rebellion from him and one day we will meet him in court. God will judge each person fairly. Some will be given what they have demanded all their lives: separation from God. This separation from all that is good is what the Bible calls hell."

Tracy looked at me blankly. *Maybe I'm talking too much,* I wondered. *Maybe she really thinks I'm an ax murderer now? . . . Oh, well, I'm in too deep.*

"Bottom line, Tracy, I believe in hell because Jesus believes in hell. He talked about it more than he did heaven. I think he did because it's a warning. He's saying to us, 'Don't go there. You don't have to if you follow me.' "

I'm not sure that my argument convinced her, but my hope was to give facts that would knock down hindrances formed naturally in her mind. In this case I wanted Tracy to know that I understood her question. I wanted to affirm that it was a good question and yet to help her see that belief in hell didn't mean you had to kiss your brains goodby. Finally, I wanted to point her to the goodness of God and the hope of Jesus.

Giving examples for all points of apologetics is beyond the scope of this book and my typing skills. Here are some responses to six of the top questions; I have taken them from Cliffe Knechtle's excellent book *Give Me an Answer* (IVP). But this format (understand; affirm; point to Christ) applies to almost any book on apologetics.

1. Aren't there many ways to God?

Understand: It sounds enlightened to ask this question. It also means that you don't have to take any religion seriously.

Affirm: Christians don't want to put down other religions. We understand that people of different faiths are sincere. There is truth in all religions.

Point to Christ: If other religions work just as well, why should Jesus die on the cross? The important point is that what opens the way to heaven is not a religious system but a person, the person of Jesus Christ. So, what do you think of Jesus' claims about how we get to God?

2. Does God really send people to hell?

Understand: It is very unpopular to believe in hell because hell seems unfair. Sometimes people ask this question on an emotional level—friends or family may have died without knowledge of Christ.

Affirm: This is a hard thing. Christians struggle with it too. At the root the question is, "Is this God you believe in a good God?"

Point to Christ: I don't know exactly what happens to individuals after they die. I do know that God is good. I also know that this goodness is what will punish evil—even evil in us. Christ brings to us the offer of an escape from judgment.

3. Why is there so much evil in the world?

Understand: This is the only apologetic, or "proof," for atheism.[1] Evil is one of the things that Christians struggle with too.

Affirm: Ultimately our answers fall short.

Point to Christ: I believe in a God on a cross, One who has suffered with us and knows our pain. For some reason, God has chosen not to wipe out all evil—and he has chosen to identify with us in our experience of it. (Perhaps it's because Jesus claims the greatest evil is rejecting him as the Christ.) Ultimately Jesus offers us more hope in dealing with the problem of evil than any secular system of philosophy does.[2]

4. How can you say Christianity is rational?

Understand: People don't want to follow something that is capricious and makes them look stupid. People have confused faith and myth.

Affirm: Appreciate the concern for truth. There seem to be many who become religious and kiss their brains goodby.

Point to Christ: All historical beliefs are based on evidence. There is enormous evidence that President Roosevelt existed. There is enormous evidence that Jesus existed and is who the Bible claims him to be. Examine the evidence for Christ.

5. Why are there so many hypocrites in the church?

Understand: People abhor insincerity. People see the atrocities committed in the name of Christ, from fractional fighting in Northern Ireland to the murder of a doctor by someone who is "pro-life."

Affirm: Most committed Christians are horrified by the way so-called Christians have used the name of Christ for their own selfish ends.

Point to Christ: This is the sin most condemned by Christ. But of course the Bible claims that all people are sinners. Hypocrisy can be found in all of us; the only one who could claim to be free from the charge of hypocrisy was Jesus.

6. Isn't the Bible full of errors?

Understand: For many people the Bible is a mysterious and strange old book. People also want to dismiss the Bible's claims on their life.

Affirm: No one wants to base their faith on an error.

Point to Christ: Internal consistency, historical consistency and archaeological evidence all suggest the Bible is one of the most reliable documents of antiquity. Read the New Testament for what it claims to be: an accurate eyewitness account of the historical Jesus Christ. Then decide for yourself who Christ was.

There are many wonderful books dealing with the objections to Christianity. Please read them. *Mere Christianity* by C. S. Lewis remains one of the best books on apologetics for the Christian faith. The new *Handbook of Christian Apologetics* by Peter Kreeft and Ronald K. Tacelli is thorough and helpful. *Give Me an Answer* by Cliffe Knechtle comes from real-life experience on the streets. Just remember, the issue is not what the answers are as much as whether we use the answers in a wise way.

Questions for Reflection or Discussion
1. What three principles govern Jesus' response to the woman's question about worship?

2. How does the discussion between Philip and the African Marxist demonstrate all three principles?

3. How does the discussion between Mack and Tracy do the same?

4. Think through a tough question you have heard or been asked (not one of the six listed at the end of the chapter). In your own words answer the question using the three guidelines: understand; affirm; point to Christ.

Pray that you'll be able to answer questions from your heart and with your mind.

• Thirteen •

Telling Our Story

Judee Marshall walked into a room and lit it up. Bright, vivacious, friendly, her presence in our fellowship was a needed spark in a rather harmless Christian group. She played the guitar. She told funny stories. She loved Christ.

When we agreed to do something scary—sponsor a campus outreach using evangelist Cliffe Knechtle—Judee was a prime mover.

Cliffe Notes

Far from giving a tame lecture about Christianity, Cliffe's style is to involve his audience. Rather than preach, Cliffe uses a question-and-answer format. He speaks for five minutes, then opens the floor to "wherever anyone is coming from."

On campus, people's questions are coming from some wild and furious places.

"Christians put my people in chains," says an angry African-American.

"Why did God command Joshua to kill all those people in the Bible?" calls out a skeptical grad student.

A philosophy major asks, "Why should I believe in Jesus and not Santa Claus?"

A sorority girl says, "That may be truth for you, but who are you to say it's truth for me?"

"What do you think about evolution?" baits a biologist.

"I'm a homosexual, and I can't believe the hatred I've gotten from the Christian church. How do you expect me to believe in Jesus?" asks a young man.

Though the crowds are sometimes hostile, all are impressed with Cliffe's answers—both the substance and the tone.

Judee had seen Cliffe in action a year before. She knew that when Cliffe comes on campus, Jesus Christ becomes an issue. That's always worthwhile and sometimes frightening. But a private decision Judee made to herself frightened her even more. Judee knew Cliffe would ask some students to give a short account of how they came to faith—to give a testimony of their experience with Christ. Judee decided to face the crowd and tell her story.

Most of the campus Christian groups were involved with the outreach. Posters went up; the campus papers carried ads. The students busied themselves with follow-up training. The day came for Cliffe to arrive, and that's when Judee told me about her decision. She wanted to share with the crowd about how she was introduced to Christ. For Judee it was a petrifying step.

Cliffe was speaking in the amphitheater. A huge crowd had formed, many wanting a shot at Cliffe. The obvious fact that Cliffe lost few arguments seemed only to fuel the furor. Judee was sitting next to me on the amphitheater's steps, and then she heard

Cliffe say, "I have a friend named Judee."

Moment of Truth

Judee's breath became so rapid that I thought she was going to hyperventilate.

"Judee is a student here at the University of Tennessee," Cliffe continued.

Judee's hands balled into fists, and her eyes were wide. Her fear became contagious as a common cold—I felt my heart rate go up too. As Cliffe continued to introduce Judee, I turned to her and said, "Judee, I have a verse for you. Remember, Jesus said if we acknowledge him before others, he will acknowledge us before his heavenly Father" (Mt 10:32 NRSV).

Judee took a breath. "Yes, that's right." Then with firmer conviction, "That's right. Thanks, Mack . . . I can do it now."

Judee stood in front of the crowd, smiled a nervous smile, said "Hi." Then she waved at the crowd. I felt like a nervous relative at a piano recital. "Lord, just help her get through," I prayed.

Judee fumbled a bit at first, but then she found her voice and gave a fine account of her faith in Christ. She said who she had been without Christ, how she had come to understand Jesus as the truth and how her life was different now with Christ.

Judee had no story of violence, sex or drugs—she came from a Christian home. But her story was unique all the same. She gave the simple old story of how, through Christ, we find true meaning and fulfillment. The masses didn't convert. But Judee honored Christ through her faithfulness.

Judee sat down, and Cliffe stood up. I'm not sure who felt more relieved, Judee or me.

The crowd took up where they had left off. "There's all these people starving in Africa, how can you say your God is a good God when he doesn't do anything about that?"

Judee and I didn't hear the questions or Cliffe's answers. She gripped my shoulder and shook me. "I did it, I did it," she said, looking straight ahead. She had a dazed look of unbelief on her face, and a big grin.

"You sure did!" I said. "You acknowledged Jesus before others."

As I looked at the crowd, I wondered about the second sentence in Jesus' declaration in Matthew: "But whoever denies me before others, I also will deny before my Father in heaven" (Mt 10:33 NRSV). *That's far more frightening,* I said to myself.

Unlikely Witness

The Samaritan woman gave a testimony, too. But who would have picked this woman to be Jesus' first evangelist?

Just then his disciples returned and were surprised to find him talking with a woman. But no one asked, "What do you want?" or "Why are you talking with her?"

Then, leaving her water jar, the woman went back to the town and said to the people, "Come, see a man who told me everything I ever did. Could this be the Christ?" (Jn 4:27-29)

A woman in Palestine couldn't even give testimony in a court of law.[1] In addition, this woman was a prostitute. She was the least of the least—and Jesus' first evangelist. That should give us hope. Long before John the evangelist became John *the* evangelist, this woman had brought her entire village to meet Jesus.

We're not surprised when she leaves her water jar. She has just finished an amazing discussion with Jesus, and she didn't come to the well for water in the first place. Her contact with Christ gives her boldness and confidence to tell others the exciting news.

When she reports to the village, notice she does not say, "Come see someone who has answered all my questions about worship." She says, "Come see a man who told me everything I ever did." Clearly the words of Jesus that had impact were the words about her life, the words that spoke to her situation. And that's what she tells others.

Notice too, she does what she can with what she has. Anyone who has met Christ can point to him. Our testimony is not so much to answer questions as it is to point to Jesus and ask people to consider, "Could this be the Christ?"

I remember sitting through one particularly bad account of a person's experience with Christ at a Christian meeting and thinking, "People don't tell of their faith out of bad motives. Most people I know have the best intentions. It's more that we haven't learned *why* we are to tell our stories and *how* to tell them well."

Here are some suggestions:

1. Know what a testimony is for.

In *Daring to Draw Near,* John White offers these thoughts (where he said *prayer,* I have inserted the word *testimony*):

If you want to learn about windows, you will do well to take a look at a few of them. The problem will be that you will not only look at, you will look through. And if your curiosity is anything like mine, the windows themselves will at times disappear.

Testimonies are like that. It is what you see through them that matters. For they are windows on eternity, looking out on the profoundest issues of life and death. Before long you forget you are dealing with a testimony, so startled are you by what you see beyond it. From time to time I have had to tap on the glass pane so that I would not forget what I was doing.[2]

We need to let our stories be windows. Then people will see through us and through our stories to Christ.

2. Keep Christ at the center. Does the story point to Christ or to you? This can be a notoriously fine line to walk. By definition a testimony is a firsthand account. We don't speak about other people's experiences; we speak about ours. The Samaritan woman simply invited people to meet a person who had made a difference in her life. It was a powerful testimony.

3. Speak truthfully. Just tell about your experience with Jesus. Don't feel pressured to twist your story based on a desire for a certain result or because of a certain theology.

Steve told me that his (very interesting) testimony was published by a national Christian magazine in a way that twisted his story. When he asked why, he was told that his story did not fit the magazine's theology and so was changed to suit their parameters. "But," Steve replied, "it's not the truth."

4. Know your *story, not someone else's.* Maybe you didn't sell guns to guerrilla groups in Guyana before you came to Christ, but that doesn't mean you have nothing to say. Your story is unique and important because it was an encounter with God, not because of the awful things you did.

Five Steps to Being a Window

Now we're down to the nitty-gritty: What, exactly, should you *say* in your testimony? Here are some ideas, taken largely from Breck and Robbie Castleman's training program for students and churches, called "The Andy Johnson Workshop." Let's use Leeann as an example for each point.

1. Start by telling what your concept of Jesus was before you met him. We do this to show that our ideas were not that different from most other people's. It elicits a "Yeah, that's what I thought about Jesus" response. Not everyone will respond that way—but if you felt a certain way about Christ, there are others who do too.

Leeann: "I was a good churchgoer. I believed that Jesus was

the Son of God, but the implications of that were fuzzy. My view of Jesus was a string of clichés: a holy, blue-eyed, angel-like figure. Jesus seemed far too religious and distant to bother with my real-life inner turmoil: Should I take honors English? What would happen to my social standing in the vicious politics of the high-school lunchroom if I didn't sit with Missy Turner? Even the deeper, unspoken terror I had of death."

2. Then say what happened that enabled you to be introduced to and trust in Jesus.

Leeann: "Then something happened in our youth group at church. Fringe people started participating. They said they had become Christians. I was offended. I had been a faithful churchgoer for years. Worse, I heard they were visiting other youth in our church and sharing with them about how they, too, could come to Christ. I dreaded being visited by these Johnny-come-latelies. I decided the best defense was a good offense: I joined them.

"One night, as we were doing 'outreach' in the home of a young woman, Ron turned to me and said, 'Leeann, why don't you tell Jane what Christ has meant to you?' I had nothing to say. I felt hollow, phony and empty. Christ was just a Sunday-school image to me. That night, back at my house, I went through the Four Spiritual Laws (the booklet we were handing out to the other students). The penny dropped: I was missing a personal relationship with Christ. There was a prayer at the end of the booklet, and so I prayed that Christ would take over my life."

3. Next say how you now grasp the truth of the gospel. This helps you clarify your past perceptions and explain what happened to change them. It also lets people know that coming to Christ begins a journey of spiritual growth.

Leeann: "Before coming to Christ I felt in the dark about spiritual things in general. But the biggest point I was missing about Christianity was that becoming a Christian meant having a relationship with Jesus."

4. Then give the life evidence of the presence of Christ. This further clarifies that we don't just come to Jesus as a one-shot deal, but that it's a lifelong relationship.

Leeann: "My new relationship with Christ freed me from the bondage of anxiety. The fact he was now in control and that he loved me gave me a tremendous release from fear. I still have worries at times, but the old terror is a burden I've not carried since."

5. Give a growing-edge account of your relationship with Jesus today.

We need to let people see that we don't become perfect by coming to Christ, but that his presence is what makes the difference.

Leeann: "My need for a Savior becomes clearer and clearer as time goes on. Christ knows what I need even if I'm out of touch. It used to be that I thought the goal was to be a better person. Today my goal is to live in the rich love of God—and so become a better lover of life and others and God. That's the point of spiritual growth for me now."

Leeann's testimony is a good example. She didn't do anything outlandish. Her "ordinary" story is something many can relate to.

Take some time to write down these five parts of your own story, in your own words. They will be different for different people, but make sure your story centers on Christ.

You Better Hold On

The summer after Judee gave her testimony, I got a call from Marty Marshall, Judee's father. I was pleased to hear from him. The Marshall family had expressed appreciation for I-V's ministry to Judee. Her parents had formed a friendship with us. Leeann and I had even housed Judee's folks during one visit to Knoxville.

I gave a cheerful hello. But Marty's reply was strained: "Mack, I've got some bad news."

I waited.

"Yesterday Judee was killed in a car wreck. We don't know all the details, but it involved a truck on I-40. She was on her way to give her testimony to a women's group . . ."

"We . . ." Marty's voice cracked. He paused to gain his composure.

". . . we would like you to speak at the funeral. We'd like for you to give a statement about what Judee stood for."

I don't know that I've ever honored a more sacred request.

At the funeral I talked about what Judee would have said. "Judee's life stood for things eternal," I said. I quoted a song she taught the campus fellowship: "Build your life on things eternal, hold to God's unchanging hand."

Students seated in the center of the church spontaneously burst out with the refrain: "You better hold on."

Surprised, I sang back the response: "You better hold on."

I talked about acknowledging Christ before others. I gave an eyewitness account of Judee's faithfulness. I said I knew what Jesus was now doing before the residents of heaven and before God the Father. He was acknowledging Judee as his faithful daughter. He was saying, "Well done, good and faithful servant" (Mt 25:21).

I think of Judee whenever I help others share their story of faith. We should never forget the spiritual realities of giving our testimony. Hold on. The story of our experience with Christ has eternal impact.

Questions for Reflection or Discussion

1. In what ways was the woman at the well an odd choice for

Jesus' first evangelist? What was her chief qualification? How does that give us hope for our own efforts in evangelism?
2. List the five steps to letting your story be a window to Christ. Write your story under each of the five steps.

Pray for an opportunity to share your story of faith.

• Part III •

How Paul Engaged His World

We are therefore Christ's ambassadors,
as though God were making his appeal through us.
We implore you on Christ's behalf: Be
reconciled to God. (2 Cor 5:20)

• Fourteen •

The Big Picture

Industrial theft in the Soviet Union during the sixties became a national scandal. Nikita Khrushchev responded in 1961 by establishing a security detail to police the pilfering.

An electronics plant in Kiev presented a particular problem. Items produced there were easily smuggled in a pocket or fold of clothing and commanded high prices on the black market. Popov, the security guard assigned at the plant, was a cheerful and winsome man—unlike many of his grim comrades in the security detail. Popov rapidly befriended the workers and after a few weeks at the Kiev plant could greet most workers by name.

At the end of one work day, Uri, a laborer, exited the plant pushing a load of sawdust in a wheelbarrow. Popov stopped him.

"Uri, what are you taking in the wheelbarrow?"

"I'm just taking this sawdust to the trash. Please," he said, waving at the load, "you may check."

Popov sifted carefully through the sawdust but found nothing.

The same thing happened the following week, and then again and again. Always there were no electronic parts, only sawdust. Finally Popov took another tack.

After stopping Uri with his now familiar load, he said, "Uri, are we friends?"

"Oh yes, Popov, we are friends."

"Then Uri, I ask you as a friend, not as a security man . . . what are you stealing?"

Uri hung his head he glanced from shoe to shoe. "Popov," he said, "since you ask as a friend, I will tell you as a friend . . . I am stealing wheelbarrows."

Paul's Overall Approach

Our look at Jesus in John 4 is a microview. One encounter with one person on one day. It's a wonderful model. But the danger with this slice-of-life view is that, just like Popov, we can miss the big picture. We can miss some broader themes of evangelism.

Paul's life gives us a big-picture view of evangelism. He was, after all, the master evangelist. Paul said that Christ had called him "to preach the gospel" (1 Cor 1:17). And his efforts at outreach took place in the nitty-gritty of life over several decades. Paul overcame enormous difficulties—physical, societal, intellectual—to tell others about Christ. And since Paul's words and actions frame biblical evangelism, no book on evangelism is complete without a look at Paul. Let's take two big-picture views of Paul.

Big Picture #1: Paul's World

Many might think that Paul's world two millennia ago wouldn't relate to ours. Yet our world has much in common with Paul's. Sure, Paul didn't have to worry about finding the right battery for his cellular phone, but just think how familiar some of his problems sound.

☐ Are you tired of being portrayed unfairly by the media? Afraid that a mention of your faith in God will lump you in with the religious kooks seen on tabloid TV?

You're not the only one to face bad press and disinformation. A first-century letter written by Pliny the Younger to the emperor implies that the Christians were being accused of being cannibals because they ate the "blood and body" of Christ in Communion. Paul was hounded by early spin doctors who wanted to use him for their own ends. It's said that Nero spread misinformation about Christians as a primitive form of spin control, to keep the people's attention off his poor leadership in government.[1]

☐ Are you unsettled by sex massage ads in the sports section? Do talk-show audiences applauding the latest trends in incest make you feel uncomfortable? Does it seem that biblical norms about human sexuality are out of sync with the culture? Do you feel if you mention that sex is holy and created by God, you'll be labeled outdated or old-fashioned?

Imagine Paul's task as he instructed the tiny church in Corinth[2] on godly sexuality. It was a hard sell—Corinth's sex massage parlors carried an international reputation,[3] and they were housed in official places of worship. It's estimated that the religious prostitutes to the goddess Diana in the temples of Corinth numbered in the thousands.[4] The believers in that congregation were even proud of an incestuous relationship between church members (1 Cor 5:1-2).

☐ Are you angered or frightened by the bill before Congress that won't allow Christians to talk about their faith in the workplace?

Imagine how the church in Ephesus felt. Industry leaders realized that if many people turned to Christ there would be a loss in idol sales and tourist dollars. A riot erupted in the marketplace and almost got Paul beat up (Acts 19:23-31).

☐ On campus have you felt "dissed" by your profs? Your English TA trotted out some old atheistic dogma, and all the class seemed to chuckle its approval.

Paul knew the feeling. He spoke to some of the world's leading intellectuals in Athens. Paul had done his homework. He quoted their own poets in response. And then Paul said, "In the past God overlooked [your] ignorance, but now he commands all people everywhere to repent. For he has set a day when he will judge the world with justice by the man he has appointed. He has given proof of this to all men by raising [Jesus] from the dead" (Acts 17:30-31).

Many of the profs at the "University of Mars Hill" only sneered and jeered. (Read all of Acts 17, for a great look at Paul on campus.)

From spin control in government to scorn on campus to outright persecution in the marketplace, Paul's situation was modern. His story helps me know I'm not alone in my frustrations with the modern world. It helps me know that the way Paul responded can relate to our world today too. If the pressures Paul faced in his world were similar to the pressures we face, Paul's responses are model responses for our world.

Big Picture #2: Paul's Worldview
Paul responded to his world out of his worldview. Paul proclaimed Christ in the chambers of kings and when he was sitting around in chains—and sometimes both were true at the same time! (Acts 26:27-29). He did not waver. He was not intimidated or cowed. He never gave up. He endured because of his steady

big-picture worldview: "That is why, for Christ's sake, I delight in weaknesses, in insults, in hardships, in persecutions, in difficulties" (2 Cor 12:10). So what was this worldview which gave Paul such tenacity and drive? In a word, *reconciliation*—the end of conflict, the end of hostility.[5]

Paul makes it clear in Romans 1—11 that once we were God's enemies, but now through Christ we have been *reconciled* to God. Many people feel that God is our "big-buddy-in-the-sky." But Paul's starting point for reconciliation was the hostility that exists between God and man. He would have agreed with his modern-day distant relative, Yitzhak Rabin.[6] Prime Minister Rabin commented wryly to critics of the West Bank peace process, "Peace is not made with friends. Peace is made with enemies."[7]

Reconciliation was the central theme of Paul's life. His whole life was wrapped around this theme. It is impossible to understand Paul, his ministry or his writings if you miss this crucial point.[8]

For Paul the theme of reconciliation takes two directions: reconciliation vertically, with God, and horizontally, with other people.

Vertical

Of primary concern for Paul was a person's relationship with Christ. Gender didn't matter (Gal 3:27-28). What you did for a living was unimportant. Your nationality, your bank account and the color of your skin were all secondary to the chief question on Paul's heart: "Do you know the gift of reconciliation through Christ? Have you made peace with God though the work of Christ?"

That's not to say Paul was a one-dimensional evangelist—a sort of memorized-gospel-outline-gone-wild. Paul adapted to situations. He could be blunt or diplomatic. Sometimes he was clever—other times he was simple. He got mad. He was tender. But at the heart of it was his desire to call others to reconcile with God.

So when Paul traveled he didn't go on a sightseeing junket. He went with reconciliation on his mind. (And are we ever glad he sent more than postcards.)

And if Paul was chained to a guard it was an opportunity to share the good news. He gave new meaning to the phrase "captive audience"—just look at the reference to the Roman guard who became a brother (Phil 4:22). (Some have noted it might be better to say a guard was chained to Paul rather than Paul to a guard.)

Or if Paul was giving prayer requests to First Church at Colossae, he didn't ask that God would find him a new job or even get him out of jail. He requested prayer that "every time I open my mouth I'll be able to make Christ plain as day to them" (Col 4:4 *The Message*).

Okay, I admit these are lofty standards . . . but that's why Paul's a model!

Horizontal

Paul didn't stop with evangelism; all relationships for Paul played out the theme of reconciliation.

So when Paul pleaded with his friends in Philippi to "agree with each other in the Lord" (Phil 4:2), it wasn't because conflict unnerved Paul. Hardly. He knew that for Christians who had been reconciled to God to be at odds with one another was unseemly—not to mention destructive to the witness of the gospel.

When Paul counseled against alcohol abuse (Rom 14:21; Eph 5:18; 1 Tim 3:8; Tit 2:3), it was not because he was a prude, but because he knew of the broken relationships alcohol abuse brought. The same could be said of overinflated egos, divorce or gossip.

Or when Paul stated how wrong it was to let ethnic differences separate believers (Gal 3:27-28), it wasn't because he wanted to be politically correct: he knew that relationships broken by ethnic hatred had slim hopes apart from a work of the Spirit.

And on it goes: husbands and wives, workers and government, people from different walks of life—to all he would say, remember, our horizontal relationships with others should parallel our vertical relationship with God.

Does this sound like more lofty standards? Well, yes, but powerful things happen when the horizontal and vertical elements of reconciliation cross.[9]

Are there some areas that need to be reconciled in your life? It's no mistake that Paul tells us of our need to be reconciled with others in the same breath as he urges us to be agents of reconciliation for others.

"We are therefore Christ's ambassadors, as though God were making his appeal through us. We implore you on Christ's behalf: Be reconciled to God" (2 Cor 5:20).

Perhaps you owe someone something—like an apology. Perhaps there's a strained relationship that should be put right. A sin that needs to be confessed. Whatever it is, lack of peace in relationships is a hindrance to sharing the gospel.

Crossover

I once saw the horizontal and vertical cross powerfully. It started at a campus Christian leadership conference.

Debra, from West Georgia College, requested prayer. "Every time I walk by the Sigma Nu house on my way to class, I pray for those guys," she said. "I wonder, how can I, a black woman, get the gospel into that place?"

Some of the students from the University of Tennessee glanced at each other. Far from the foreign territory Debra sensed about the Sigma Nu house, the UT students saw it as a comfortable place. Robb whispered, "Eric hangs out at the Sigma Nu house all the time; he almost pledged Sigma Nu. We can get into the Sigma Nu house. Our problem is how to get into the black cultural center."

So started a reconciliation event—horizontal and vertical.

The Christian student leaders from UT, mostly white, got together with the leaders from West Georgia, mostly African-Americans, and made a covenant. "We'll come to your campus and do outreach with you, and then you come to our campus and do outreach with us."

Late that fall UT traveled to Georgia. Alex, the staffworker for West Georgia, gave some simple instructions for our first day of outreach: "One student from West Georgia pair up with a student from UT. Spend some time getting to know each other. Then just walk around campus with the gospel on your hearts and see what God does."

Alex grinned at me and repeated, "Let's just see what the Lord does." He knew this approach was very different from my "white" decency-and-order mode. He also knew this approach was effective.

The Big Test

Debra, the woman who started the whole thing, was paired with me. Before the group dispersed we milled nervously in front of the student center. Debra procrastinated by talking to some friends in the group. Just "seeing what the Lord might do" can be unnerving!

As I waited for Debra to finish her conversation, I leaned on an enormous old Cadillac parked by the curb. I felt self-conscious. For the first time in my life I was in a white-majority situation where all my friends—the only people I knew on campus—were African-American. Both whites and blacks stared at us. I realized with a shock that our black brothers and sisters faced ostracism from the African-American community by just being with us. "Lord, thank you for the risk they are taking. Make it worth it," I prayed.

No sooner had I settled on the headlight than I noticed the car wasn't empty—two young women sat inside staring at us. I sprang off their car and said a guilty hello. But they weren't interested in what propped me up—they were interested in our group. The driver addressed me while still staring at the crowd in front of the student center. "What's going on here?" she said in a thick Scandinavian accent.

"Well," I said, "it's a long story"—I then remembered Alex's admonition to look for what the Lord was doing—"but a good one. Do you want to hear about it?"

"Yes," both women said in unison. They motioned for me to get in.

I jumped into the back seat of the Caddie. I felt as if I was in somebody's living room. The worn seats were upholstered in a thick, gold, couchlike cloth.

They were exchange students. The car was on loan from the university—a tax write-off from a wealthy Georgian.

I said, "So don't tell me, let me guess, you're wondering why this racially mixed group is standing in front of a student center in the deep South acting like great friends?" (I decided to skip the part about procrastinating.)

"Well, yes," they confessed. "We've not seen any racially mixed groups since we've been in America."

I saw Debra craning her neck for me. I called to her. When she spotted me waving from the back seat of that old gold chariot, she cocked her head and gave me a sideways raised-eyebrow look. I motioned for her to join me while I continued talking to the international students. Debra approached the car looking bemused but eased herself into the back seat when she heard our conversation.

"Debra and I are here out of our belief in reconciliation," I said. It was Paul's party line, straight out of Colossians. "God is in the business of reconciling relationships. He offers peace through his blood, shed on the cross."

Debra, though confused on how I'd wound up in the back seat of the car, held no confusion about the gospel. "That's right," she jumped in. "We believe that God is reconciling the world. Reconciliation between people who might not normally get along . . . and more importantly, reconciling people with himself."

Wow! Debra spoke with power. She told them how she had come to faith in Christ. She talked about Christ as the center of her life. The exchange students were mesmerized. It was not the last time I have regretted the power and wisdom the church in America has lost by being segregated.[10]

Out of the car and out of earshot, Debra asked, "How in the world did you get in that car?" And she added, "I wasn't expecting God to work quite *that* powerfully." There's power in reconciliation.

That was a common thought among the rest of the students too. Sharing the gospel seemed more powerful together. (It makes sense: we were talking about being reconciled to God while demonstrating reconciliation together.)

The impact of our exchange continues to this day: a prayer meeting started at the black cultural center at UT and a new Christian fellowship at Knoxville College, a historically black campus in Knoxville. Friendships were formed, eyes were opened, hearts were changed—some people even accepted

Christ. What started as a concern to bring the good news to a frat house became a bigger picture, a more powerful event.

That's because a concern for reconciled relationships, both horizontal and vertical, touches the very heart of God. Just as Paul knew it did, centuries before.

Questions for Reflection or Discussion

1. How are Paul's world and ours similar?

2. What different facets are there in our vertical reconciliation with God?

3. What different facets are there in our horizontal reconciliation with others?

Pray that God will show you one area of vertical reconciliation and one area of horizontal reconciliation that you might practice now.

• Fifteen •

Ambassadorship

Years ago, when "multimedia" meant a fancy slide show, my staffworker, Bill Christensen, would lug a big electronic gizmo to our weekly campus meetings. The "Pocket Star" covered two desktops. Its full-sized projectors and cassette deck were built into a hard-sided suitcase. The cassette player gave sound to the slides and silent instructions to a primitive computer. The computer started the show, advanced the slides, and faded the images in and out.

Bill would point the Pocket Star at the smoothest section of cinder block we could find in the student center. Then Bill would ease himself back for the show—at least for a time.

The shows were about discipleship, missions and evangelism. The actual productions are now faded memories. The really interesting thing about the Pocket Star was that occasionally a

---

slide would get stuck in the projector. The tape would continue to turn while Bill burst into angry motion. He would rattle the projector to unstick the slide and then manually advance the slide tray to match the tape.

Invariably this meant the show was off a slide or two. Ironic images would appear: Samuel Escobar speaking with Elisabeth Elliot's voice, jet airplane sounds coming from the mouth of an international student. We always looked forward to watching shows with the Pocket Star (and Bill) at our weekly meetings.

One production did stick with me despite the early glitches of multimedia. The show was called "The Effective Ambassador" and was based on a talk by Paul Little.

The show started with Little's voice quoting a passage of Scripture from 2 Corinthians 5:18, 20: "The apostle Paul says, 'All this is from God, who reconciled us to himself through Christ and gave us the ministry of reconciliation . . . We are therefore Christ's ambassadors'!"

First slide: typical "John Student" sitting at his desk in his college dorm. He responds to this thought with a befuddled "who, me?" expression.

Little's voice in the background continues verse 20: (drum roll) "as though God were making his appeal *through us.*"

Next frame (rim shot): John Student again, magically re-dressed in tuxedo, red sash, medals and white gloves. His expression has changed: wonder is on his face as he inspects his new ambassadorial duds. He takes a dignified Napoleonesque stance.

Little's voice finishes the segment with, "When you sit and drink coffee with someone and you get right down to the crucial issue of a person's relationship with Christ and you invite them to the Savior, have you ever thought you are the last link on a chain that stretches from the very throne of God, that God literally *makes his appeal through you* to that person? Have you ever realized that you are an ambassador for the foreign policy of the kingdom of heaven?"

Paul Little's image of an ambassador was perfect. It was the apostle Paul's way of putting feet on his theme of reconciliation. He used it to give the young church at Corinth a practical model from real life. (It's not like he could draw on the history of the church.) Just think of the rich parallels between Christians and ambassadors.

Paul knew his flock could respond to the growing hostility toward Christians in a variety of ways. The same kinds of options, we have noted, face *us* today: the holy huddle, brittle combat, or simple assimilation into the culture. Yet Paul wanted Christians to avoid these extremes and be *available* to the world around them (remember the job description).

Me? An Ambassador?

In Paul's day an ambassador was chosen by the king, commissioned by the highest powers of the land, entrusted with a message and sent with full honors.

Paul says that's who we are: chosen, commissioned, given a message and sent. Like it or not—whether we know it or not—as we go through life, we are ambassadors to those we meet around us. The question, as Paul sees it, is not "Should I be an ambassador?" but "In what ways can I be a better ambassador?"

Here are some parallels between the image of an ambassador and the Christian as an ambassador.

☐ Ambassadors are public people. They know their actions can discredit their message. So they act in ways to give credit and weight to the message they carry.

We are public people too. Many Christians act as though they are undercover agents, but Scripture tells us to live out our faith

164

privately *and* publicly. Actions speak.

Four summers ago, Leeann and I bought our house in Lexington. We were excited about our new home—except for one glitch. We were leaving the day after the papers were signed, to direct the short-term program in Kenya. We didn't have enough time to move our furniture from our apartment.

Two friends, David and Angie McNeill, volunteered to get the task done during the two months we were gone. It was a wonderful service of love to us. But it was also an act of ambassadorship to my sister Linda.

Linda watched David and Angie move our stuff, and she puzzled over what it meant. *Why?* she thought. *Why in the world would people love each other like that?* Those thoughts grew to even bigger questions: *What would it be like to have friends who loved you that much?* Ultimately her thoughts became, *What would it feel like to have unconditional love for others?*

Then the Spirit spoke to her heart, "They're all Christians." It sounded like her own thoughts, but it was the Spirit. That idea was a critical link for my sister: within the year Linda would accept Christ.

David and Angie were ambassadors between Christ and my sister by living out their Christian love and faith in an open and public way. Their public actions gave credit to their message.

☐ Ambassadors avoid disqualifications. Certain things can disqualify an ambassador. The ambassador knows, for instance, that if he or she becomes a citizen of the foreign power, that means being disqualified from the post. The ambassador never forgets the homeland.

Christians are citizens of another kingdom first, and citizens of our earthly nation second.[1] Assimilation into the culture is a disqualification.

There are other things that disqualify ambassadors: not delivering the message, for example, or tampering with the message's content. The ambassador's friendship with the king is no excuse for changing the message. Indeed, ambassadors are, at times, in the dark about the underlying purposes and strategies of the king and the message. Their job is not to make strategies for the kingdom or provide enforcing muscle, but to deliver the message as given.

Sometimes I'm tempted to tamper with the message: to drop the hard parts and soften the rough edges of Christ's words. (Picking up crosses and being thrown into lakes of fire come to mind.) Some succumb to this temptation in a big way.

Recently a major denomination in our area ran full-page ads showing pictures of Dante's inferno. The ad touted, "You won't get fire and brimstone at our churches."

Understand, I abhor the gleeful expositions of hell some are prone to give ("I've got good news! You're going to hell!"). And relevant Christianity is a passion for me. But I'm not for selling out. Selling out to Madison Avenue, for one; it was a full-page ad. I'm not for putting down other churches to increase declining membership for another. But the saddest thing about this ad was its open declaration that they would not even grapple with, much less teach, something Jesus taught: judgment is real.

No, tampering with the message is a disqualification. We may know volumes about the message, we may know the message giver—but we do not know his ultimate aims and plans, so we are not free to tamper with the message we are given. The ambassador, then, has a dilemma.

☐ Every ambassador, at some time, must deliver hard words: issue warnings, defend actions, give understanding. He or she can't alter or refuse to relay the message.

Yet ambassadors want to appeal to people, not bash them with tough talk. An ambassador, by definition, is someone who mediates between two powers. Ambassadors want people to agree, not just hear the hard truth. Ambassadors are expected to help powers get along—they reconcile, they don't just prophesy doom. To be both truthful and appealing is not always an easy task. Some resort to manipulation. It's no wonder manipulation is sometimes called the disease of ambassadors (and evangelists). Yet the answer is not manipulation. The answer is diplomacy.

The Need for Diplomacy

Today many Christians seem willing to say the hard things in hard ways (hard-guys). Others are forever saying nice things in nice ways (goody-two-shoes). But what's needed are more diplomats—people skilled at saying the hard things in nice ways (ambassadors). People who say, "You must take this seriously," but with a smile . . . at a fancy party.

We must be able to negotiate so there is not ill will but reconciliation. Diplomacy exists to reconcile conflicts between worlds. It's an art.

So we draw on our diplomatic skills in evangelism. These are skills we saw Jesus model for us in previous chapters. Ambassador skills involve knowing the recipient culture: the language and customs of the foreign culture we're sent to. We listen humbly to others, to the Scripture, to the Holy Spirit. We're ready with understanding answers about hard things; we even apologize if appropriate.

I have found a helpful rule of thumb to use in Christian diplomacy. If we want people to take us seriously, we must take them seriously—even in things we may think are spurious and trivial.

Leeann and I made the move to Kentucky to develop groups of Christian students on Kentucky campuses. We felt called. We were full of vigor and high expectations. It was exciting just thinking about the wonderful things God had in store for us.

But our first outreach meeting at the University of Kentucky failed miserably. Twelve people showed for our Christian concert during the first week of school, and that's counting the staff families.

We decided we needed to be better diplomats. We needed to ask more questions, learn more about the culture. We wanted to use the culture's language rather than fight it. We wanted to say our message *and* be heard. We wanted to take these Kentucky college students seriously.

After some careful research, we discovered a shared-value system that permeated the UK subculture. A system so dominant and pervasive in the campus community that it produced agreement across socioeconomic boundaries. It transcended race and class. It was beyond young and old. It was a system that brought unanimity across academic disciplines and even religious disputes. It was "island-absolute" in a sea of pluralism. It was basketball.

Here was a case for a diplomat. On the one hand, we didn't want to play "Christian referee," handing out technical fouls: "Basketball is just a game, it isn't going to meet your deepest longings—only Jesus can . . ." On the other hand, that is true. That's the message we bear.

So in the spring we hosted another event. We orchestrated a week of skits, speakers and music. Our aim was to present to the campus the good news. The high point? The NCAA basketball tournament, "March Madness." After all, ambassadors throw parties, lots of them. So our diplomatic solution was to throw a basketball party.

We made plans to show the regional semifinals—held in New Orleans—on two projection TVs in the UK dorm complex. (We just assumed that UK would be in the semis.) We invited the campus. We set up hundreds of chairs. We prayed. We made free popcorn. Christian students prepared skits for the commercial breaks. We set up our halftime show—a relevant and fun presentation of the gospel.

It was standing room only. The students cheered as UK stomped Wake Forest, then hushed to watch the Christian students perform their six-part skit on "The Meaning of Life."

That night two local TV stations came and reported on our group. Channel 27, the CBS affiliate, used our gathering as a live feed into their nightly news. "Sam," the reporter said in her well-modulated TV voice, "this group is different than some watching basketball tonight. They're here promoting Christianity." Then she interviewed Jeremy, one of our first-year students. "Oh, Lord," I prayed as she poked the mike in his face, "don't let him say that 'Jesus is number one.' "

Jeremy made a great ambassador. Jeremy grinned into the camera and started with, "We're doing this because we want to make Jesus Christ as big an issue on this campus as basketball."

It was an ambassadorial coup. Jeremy summarized what we wanted everyone to understand. Basketball (contrary to local opinion) is just a game; there are some who think Jesus is more important. Sure, basketball is fun, but it is not truth—it doesn't solve life's problems; only Jesus can do that. That's the truth, with a smile.

The ambassador is a chosen and commissioned representative of the King of kings. The ambassador is given a message and sent. Ambassadors act in ways to give credit and weight to the message they carry. They avoid disqualifications; they practice the art of diplomacy. That's the Christian ambassador.

Questions for Reflection or Discussion
1. Paul Little asks the question (based on 2 Cor 5:20) "Did you

ever realize that you are an ambassador for the foreign policy of the kingdom of heaven?" List the parallels between political ambassadorship and Christian ambassadorship.

2. What strengths do you have in kingdom diplomacy? Where could you grow?

3. Are there parts of the gospel message you are tempted to skip or modify? How might diplomacy help?

Pray for an opportunity to be a Christian ambassador this week.

• Sixteen •

Immigration

John Kanga and I bumped across the south end of the Ngong Hills of Kenya. Then his car wheezed over the last incline, and the beauty of the Rift Valley swept away all concerns about the rough ride. The broad, flat tops of giant acacia trees joined together to form a green carpet below us. An occasional giraffe poked its head through the mat. John's car reached speeds his engine could never produce without the help of gravity as we began our long descent into the valley.

John called his car a miracle car, and I agreed. How in the world it continued to roll mile after African mile was a miracle. Its decade-long labors had carried John to countless villages and hamlets.

John taught in a veterinary college, but his heart ached to tell kids about Christ. So at every chance he packed his guitar in his miracle car and traveled to meet with grass-roots Christian groups in schools. The groups were called Christian Unions (CUs).

We were bound for Magadi, where I was to speak at the local high school. I had spoken to Kenyan youth groups often, but this was my first time there. John said it was a hard place.

As we drove, I got a wonderful feeling God was going to do something powerful that day. I sensed Jesus' closeness.

The acacia trees thinned. Beads of sweat rolled down our foreheads in the valley heat. There were no more jolts on the road. The asphalt now served only to point the way; the flats all around us were just as smooth as the road.

From miles away I saw Magadi poke through the level horizon. The town didn't fit. Most of the buildings were high, sterile concrete complexes built to house government workers. John told me the town existed to harvest salt. I saw the salt pits stretching for miles on either side of the road—crusty lakes of dirty, pink salt baked by the heat. They formed a low-level moat at the edge of town.

In the city center, odd combinations of modern and traditional played with my senses—Maasai nomads drank Cokes while leaning against a concrete high-rise. It was a scruffy place, but even that didn't dampen my spirits. God was up to something; I could feel it.

Surprise Results

We got to town just as school let out. The students in the CU gathered everyone they could bring to the meeting. There were two hundred students in a room built for twenty-five: kids on the floor, kids sitting on each other's laps, kids looking in through the windows. They wanted to sing with John and hear the guy from America.

John's dog-eared guitar case bore the marks of his travels, but his guitar was polished and oiled. It glistened as he pulled it out, and the students roared their approval. When John plays his guitar he always reminds me of Buddy Holly. He's good.

After a time, John gave me a gracious introduction as the speaker. "Preach with power, brother," he whispered to me before he sat down.

And I did. The students hung on every word.

At the end of my talk I said, "If God has spoken to your heart tonight, don't delay. Come to Christ. Those who would like to receive Christ, gather with me here, now, and I'll tell you how." John strummed the guitar. I braced myself for the rush.

Isn't it strange how God works? How what we want to see happen is not always what God wants to happen? How what we think is powerful is not always what God thinks is powerful?

Nobody moved. Nobody! I repeated myself. I shifted back and forth on my feet. I felt awkward and dumb. After scanning the crowd, John repeated that anyone who wanted to talk to me or him about coming to Christ could talk to us. Then he dismissed the group. I was stunned.

As the students dispersed, John came over to me and said the CU leadership wanted to talk to him about some organizational things; he would meet with them for a while before we left. He turned to go, then turned back and touched my elbow. "It's a hard place, Mack," he said.

I went out to the courtyard beside the school. The hard-packed orange clay was a great place to kick dirt. I prayed; they weren't nice prayers. "God, I feel like the biggest fool . . . I didn't say a thing those kids could understand . . . John should have spoken today, not me. Why did you send me all this way to . . ."

But then I sensed someone beside me. I turned, embarrassed that somebody might have overheard me grumbling to God.

"Hello," said a young man.

"Hello," I replied. I extended my hand.

He took my hand. "My name is Robert." He looked down at the dust. "What you talked about in there . . . I would like to have it."

"Okay, Robert," I said, "let's talk."

Robert seemed quiet, reflective. I went through the same outline I always go through: God, People, Christ, Response, Cost. I even asked Robert if he understood the cost. I'm a bit embarrassed about that now. As we talked it was clear that Robert had heard this before.

"Would you like to accept Christ now?" I asked.

"Yes," he said quietly.

Then, almost as an afterthought, I asked, "Robert, you seem to know most of what it means to become a Christian. What has held you back from accepting Christ in the past?"

Robert looked down at the clay. He made circles in the dust with his foot. "My father has told me that if I become a Christian he will beat me. Tonight . . . I will bleed."

I lifted my hand off his shoulder. It was as if someone had just hit *me*. I'm even more embarrassed by my next thoughts than by my grumpy prayers. I thought of saying, "Well, then . . . we can wait, you can do it later . . . maybe it's not worth it."

No sooner had my hand left his shoulder than I heard God's voice. Not an audible voice. It was clearer than that. "Mack, don't forget what I did so this young man could come to me."

"Yes, Lord," I said.

I prayed a simple prayer with Robert. I talked with him about following Christ. I prayed for his father. John's meeting finished, and I introduced Robert to the other CU leadership and John. Then John and I left. I haven't seen Robert since.

On the ride back to Ngong, I could scarcely see the beauty of Africa. I couldn't get my encounter with Robert and God out of my mind. I had just met a young man who knew more courage and had counted more cost than I had in my whole life. I felt humbled by Robert. I am honored to have met him.

Crossing over the Line

The Lord did do something powerful, just as I suspected. But he didn't do it the way I thought he would. No revival fell on Magadi, as I had hoped. But a young man made a powerful and courageous decision to turn to Christ. The work in my heart was powerful, too—just how committed was I to asking someone to cross over the line?

May I make a very unpopular observation? When Paul talked to people about Jesus, his aim was to *convert* them. Furthermore, if you want to share your faith with a friend, you too, must be committed to bringing about his or her *conversion*.

I know, I know. You're thinking that it's God who wills and works in someone's heart. You're thinking that it is the Holy Spirit who calls to people and touches their hearts and even gives them the faith to come to Christ. You're thinking that Paul himself couldn't convert anyone, so certainly we can't . . . and you're right. We can't convert anyone—it is the Holy Spirit's job; I haven't forgotten my words in chapter three. But our aim is to turn people to Christ. Our goal is that they will be converted.

It's surprising, but when Paul used the word *convert* (or *turn*, as it's translated in the NIV) he uses it as a reference to himself, not to the Holy Spirit as we would expect.[1]

Listen to Paul as he stands before King Agrippa in chains, explaining what Christ said to him: "I am sending you [Paul] to them to open their eyes and turn [convert] them from darkness to light, and from the power of Satan to God, so that they may receive forgiveness of sins and a place among those who are sanctified by faith in me" (Acts 26:17-18).

Evangelism is a process of opening eyes and turning people to God.

Let me quote J. I. Packer here: "Evangelizing includes the endeavor to elicit a response to the truth taught. It is communication with a view to conversion. It is a matter not merely of informing, but also of invitation. It is an attempt to gain, or win, or catch . . ."[2]

We must do that by asking people to cross over the line. Yes, this is scary, but it is part of the work of ambassadors—it's immigration work.

The word *convert,* like *sin,* is fraught with negative meanings—converting heathen at the points of spears and so on. Start by not using the word *convert; turn* has the same sort of meaning.

The deeper issue, really, is not the word but the cultural expectations. We live in an age of pluralism, the same worldview that brought us pop-religious ideas like "All religions end up at the same place" and "What's truth for you may not be truth for me."

Pluralism calls for tolerance of others' different beliefs—and sometimes for moderation of our own beliefs. That's important and needed, relationally and ethnically. But when it comes to truth—religious truth—it's a disaster. Acceptance of people is important, but tolerance is a very low biblical value. We're not called to be tolerant of injustice or untruth. Jesus says he is the way, the truth and the life, and no one comes to God except through him. That's not a particularly tolerant view. Jesus states that truth is not what is true-for-you, but what *he* says is true.

Paul called people to convert because Jesus is the truth for all people, not just truth for Paul. To ask for conversion means that we must ask someone to accept an absolute: Jesus. The aim to convert someone is an in-your-face attitude toward pluralism that sets us against culture.[3]

Pluralism presents some powerful challenges to asking people to turn to Christ. But, as my encounter with Robert reminded me, we must not forget what Jesus did for people to come to him. We stake our lives on the truth of our message, and if it's true, it's worth it.

Calling people to turn to Christ is not a license to be manipulative or rude (see the code of ethics for evangelism in appendix three). It simply means we must ask people to respond. We need to ask sensitively, humbly, with love, whether someone would like help in coming to Christ. "Jim [or Jan], would you like to step over the line and give your life to Christ?"

Flashback

Last year I attended our short-term missions banquet. Jeannie Musick, the current director of the Kenya program, got up to speak. It had been two years since my last trip to Kenya, so I was excited to hear the news.

At the conclusion of her talk, Jeannie said, "I would like to close with a story about the impact we have been having over the years with our short-term project in Kenya. This past summer I was in a small town in the middle of the Rift Valley, called Magadi."

My head snapped up.

"I spoke to the Christian group there, and afterwards a young man came up to me and asked if I knew a man with the names Mack and Stiles."

People smiled and murmured at the African way of saying American names, but my heart was in my throat.

Jeannie continued, " 'Yes,' I said, 'I know Mack very well.' "

"This young man told me his name was Robert. Then he said, 'Two years ago Mack Stiles was with us. He spoke to us about the Lord and he led me to Jesus. Would you please send greetings to him? Tell him that I am still walking with the Lord.' "

Jeannie continued, "This young man is now a leader in the Christian Union in his school and he is a testimony . . ."

Many saw my tears, but no one, including Jeannie, knew why. I had seen many come to Christ in Kenya, but only one young man in Magadi. One young man who taught me about courage, and faith, and commitment. One young man the Lord used to remind me of the cost and the value of inviting people to cross over the line.

Questions for Reflection or Discussion

1. What holds you back from asking people to step into faith in Christ?

2. How do you see in Robert's story both the need and the risk of asking people to cross over the line?

Pray that God will give you courage and then opportunities to ask people to step over the line into faith in Christ.

• Seventeen •

Establishing Residency

Paul's ministry was rooted in the meaning of the gospel.[1] So for Paul, evangelism and discipleship had a closer link than for many today—they were two parts of one process. His desire was to see people won to Christ (Rom 5:18), then to see them become one in Christ (Gal 3:26-28) by becoming a part of the family of God (Gal 6:10). When people came to Christ, they were Paul's spiritual children. Paul would often use the image of a parent when he spoke of his relationship with the new churches—both motherly love and fatherly encouragement.[2] Paul meant it when he said, "We were gentle among you, like a mother caring for her little children" (1 Thess 2:7). That's why new Christians are often called baby Christians.

Do you know what to do with a baby Christian? Baby Christians are like real babies: they're messy and they need lots of tenderness. We can't assume that they'll live happily ever after on their own. They need more than just getting born; they need care.

Paul's comment to the Thessalonians is just as true today as it was then: "We loved you so much that we were delighted to share with you not only the gospel of God but our lives as well, because you had become so dear to us" (1 Thess 2:8).

Here's my "Top Ten" list of ways you can share your life with a new believer.

1. When someone comes to Christ, ask him or her to pray for you. Part of that is selfish—when new Christians pray, powerful things happen. But it also lets them know they have a part in the body of Christ. And be sure to pray for them. New Christians will face doubts, temptations, depressions, decisions about life-styles—the list is endless, and they need prayer. It's no mistake that Paul prayed "night and day . . . most earnestly" for the church in Thessalonica (1 Thess 3:10)—the youngest church he wrote to.

2. Call or write. If you can meet together on a regular basis, do it. Keep up contact. And whether you write or meet face to face, do more than knock out a dry ten-point sermon outline.

Let people know what an important decision it is they have made. Paul did.

And let people know that they matter. They will see God in you when you do. People mattered to Paul, and it showed in his letters (in Roman 16 Paul took the time to greet twenty-seven people by name).[3] And what letters! He didn't write about the weather. His letters were filled with loving encouragement for new believers—an important ingredient for growth. Paul spoke of his "intense longing" to see the believers (1 Thess 2:17). He spoke of his constant prayers for them with joy (Phil 1:4) and the depth of his love for them (2 Cor 2:4).

3. Paul often referred to himself as a model.[4] "I urge you to imitate me," he said to the Corinthians (1 Cor 4:16). Some take offense at these words of Paul, as if he were stuck-up. But who else was he going to use as a model for Gentile believers living in a Gentile world? Socrates? Besides it was expected in Paul's day for children to imitate their parents, and Paul saw himself as their spiritual father (1 Cor 4:15).

Imitate Paul: revive the art of mentoring. Tell new believers what it means to pray and do devotional reading of Scripture. Tell them about your successes and failures in the faith. Share about your personal prayer life (the good, the bad and the ugly).

Some of Paul's first efforts with new Christians were to help them understand the implications of their new faith. Let Paul help you do the same. Buy the new Christian a Bible, then read together the stuff Paul wrote.[5]

4. Then help the new Christian understand how to use the Bible in two ways: with the mind and with the heart. The *study* of Scripture is a strength to the *mind*. Have a Bible study together. Use a study guide if it's helpful—I would recommend *Basic Christianity* by John Stott (the Bible study guide, though the book by that title is wonderful too).

The *devotional* use of the Scriptures is a strength for the *heart*. Do a month of directed quiet times with the new Christian. "Directed" means someone walks you through each quiet time step by step. Steve and Jackie Eyre's Spiritual Encounter Guides (IVP) do that in a fresh and helpful way.

5. Don't just give them an address for a church. Take them to church or a fellowship meeting or both. Paul dragged people around with him all the time. It was a great discipling tool. He was constantly involving people in the work of the church. (It's estimated, by adding all the names of people associated with Paul in the New Testament, that there were some one hundred

people who ministered alongside him.[6]) Imitate Paul and take people along.

Think through the new believer's needs in worship. Needs will be different depending on the person's background, temperament and lifestyle. A person from a highly liturgical background will have different needs from someone from a Pentecostal background. Look for a "seeker-friendly" church—most have programs for the new Christian. Introduce them to the pastor. (One exception: when a young person comes to Christ from a family that attends church, I usually recommend that he or she stay with that "faith tradition" as a witness to the family.)

6. Help them think through the meaning of the lordship of Christ in their life. Study Scripture about issues that are going to face them—work, marriage, finances or whatever. As part of being disciples, they will need to understand baptism. This is especially important for internationals since they may not have this opportunity after they return home.

When Paul and the early church struggled through what to do with the first Gentile Christians, they agreed that some warnings were urgently needed (Acts 15:19-21). We should do the same. Be willing to explain sin and its damaging effects.

Be especially aware of sins that have become patterns. Sexual sins and sins associated with other religious activities opposed to Christ (such as occult practices) should be confronted.

Help them deal with the other end of the spectrum. False guilt can be just as damaging. Tell them about the security of their salvation. First John 1:9 should be one of the first verses a new believer learns: "If we confess our sins, he is faithful and just and will forgive us our sins and purify us from all unrighteousness."

7. Some of the most delightful opportunities for sharing the gospel come to new believers. That's because they have lots of

contact with the non-Christian world. Help them talk to some of their non-Christian friends. Help them with some basic theology. Help them with some basic apologetics. Cliffe Knechtle's book and video series, *Give Me an Answer,* is a helpful start. Articulating the gospel to others will give them deeper understanding of what has happened in their own life. Give them this book for a start on speaking of Jesus.

8. Have caution for any relationship across gender lines. Coming to Christ is an intimate experience and easily confused with romance. The best rule of thumb is to let women disciple women, and men disciple men. No matter what, discipling relationships should be thought of as familial, not romantic. If you are attracted to a person who is a new Christian, or there is any possibility that they could be attracted to you, it's in the best interest for both of you to let someone else disciple them.

9. Get them reading. In case you haven't noticed by now, I like John White's book *The Fight* to help new Christians grow. There's a helpful study at the end of each chapter.

Read older stuff too. Christian history didn't start with C. S. Lewis. Start a dead theologians society. Meet in secret and read Augustine, Bernard of Clairvaux, Jeremy Taylor, John Wesley and others. They wrote some great stuff about God.

10. If you have reason to believe there has been some kind of serious trauma in someone's life in the past, such as physical, sexual or chemical abuse, that person may need Christian counseling. Know when the problem goes beyond your skill as a friend, and help the person find professional help.[7]

These ten things will help new believers establish their citizenship in the kingdom.

Who knows, one day you may find yourself part of a process that helps bring someone to faith in Christ . . . like my friend Mike.

Mike's Story

Mike, a sophomore at UK, always seems to show up at mealtime. He's good-looking, a young Christian and a classic Generation Xer.

"Well, at least I finished the manuscript of your book," Mike said as he plopped the dog-eared pages on the kitchen table.

"Great," I said as I pulled the pizza from the oven. "What did you think?"

"I really liked your stories—it's going to help lots of people." A pause. "But it's not for me." Mike perched on our kitchen windowsill and crossed his arms.

"What do you mean?"

"Well, I guess it's for people who are more spiritual than me."

"Well, Mike, that shakes me some . . . I want people who aren't religious to be able to read this stuff."

Mike looked at the pizza. "Pizza looks good," he remarked. Then he said, "I guess I just can't imagine me doing something like sharing my faith on a beach or anything."

I said, "Actually, the pizza looks smaller since you showed up; why don't we slap some burgers on too."

"Okay, I'll eat anything," he said.

Then I said, "I don't know how spiritual it was to go to the beach."

"Well, you'll see what I mean when you read my comments on the manuscript. I hope you don't mind, but my friend Terry wrote on it some too."

"No, I don't mind. Who's Terry?" I asked.

"Oh, just a friend. We worked in Colorado together this summer. Some of your stuff really made her mad, so don't be offended."

I said, "Don't worry—I'd only be offended if she said she was bored."

"She wasn't bored, that's for sure." Mike stared at the pizza while I sliced it. "It really only got her angry at first, but after she finished the manuscript it really affected her. Like, she went back to Chicago and went to talk to this pastor in a real active church. She's on a canoe trip with them this weekend even." Mike paused. "Like, she even got baptized." Mike said that as if it were really strange.

"Like, what?" I roared. Mike looked at me blankly. "Mike, it sounds as if Terry became a Christian!"

He looked up at the ceiling. "Yeah, I guess it does."

I pointed my pizza slicer at his face. "Are you telling me that God used you to help bring someone to Christ?" Mike was staring at the globs of tomato sauce on my pizza cutter, while he edged away from it. "Are you telling me that God used you in evangelism?"

"Well, I never thought of it that way."

"You never thought of it that way!?" I howled. I grabbed the baggy thermal underwear that he wears for a shirt. "Mike, you bonehead, don't tell me it's not for you when you *did* it!"

He grinned at me sheepishly. "I didn't do anything."

"That's just my point! We don't have to have it all together to share our faith. We just need to take some steps where we are. You gave her the manuscript, didn't you?"

"Well, yeah."

"Mike, that's great news."

"Yeah, I guess it is," he said. "Hey, you remember that book you gave me called *The Fight?*"

I nodded knowingly. "You want to give it to Terry, don't you?"

"No," he said. "I was hoping you could give me another copy. I just want to read it again."

I said, "What did you do with the last copy I gave you?"

"I dunno." He shrugged.

I said, "I think I gave my last copy to my sister, but let me check." I shouted at him from the other room while I scanned my bookshelf, "Maybe you could let Terry read it too?"

"Yeah, that's a good idea," he said.

Returning to the kitchen, I said, "Here's my last copy. Don't lose it."

Believe me, if Mike could be a part of someone's coming to Christ, it could happen to you. You never know how the Spirit will surprise you.

Questions for Reflection or Discussion

1. Which of the top ten discipling hints do you feel most able to do? Least able?

2. What was missing in Mike's view of evangelism?

Ask God to allow you the privilege of helping a new believer grow in his or her relationship to Christ.

• Epilogue •

Of Model A's
and
Evangelism

When I was a teen, my father bought a rusted-out 1930 Model A Ford for us to restore together. It still sits in my garage. Off and on over the years, I'd pull out the manual, study it and then work on the car. The instructions and illustrations made replacing a head gasket look like an easy task.

The actual practice of replacing a head gasket was somewhat different. Unlike the pictures of happy people replacing neat car parts, I often lacked the right tools, my parts (when I could find them) were never neat, and often the work took strange, messy and frustrating turns. But after some time I noticed I was learning more from working on the car than I did from the manual. Maybe that's what Dad had in mind.

This book comes with a twin hope. I hope it challenges you and equips you to speak of Jesus to those around you. But I recognize that, just like my Model A manual, a book cannot prepare you for the messy, puzzling and frustrating task of sharing your faith. Actual practice will teach you far more than reading a manual. And only as you practice will your confidence build.

My Model A looks a lot better now than when I first got it. It even works, on occasion. Your efforts to share your faith will work too, when you take some steps. I bet it won't even take you twenty years, as it did for me. So jump on in. See what God does. Speak of Jesus to reach your world.

Appendix 1
2 PLUS

My commitment to pray for the conversion of two friends and for boldness in taking opportunity to witness to them.

Objectives
☐ To strengthen prayer on campus or in my church
☐ To challenge us to participate with the Holy Spirit in the conversion of two of our friends
☐ To pray for boldness in our witness

Steps to live out
☐ Acknowledge dependence on God's grace to draw my friends to Christ.
☐ Identify two not-yet-Christians for whom I will pray.
☐ Develop a friendship with them.
☐ Choose a prayer partner and pray together for my friends.

While I pray, I build my friendship through
☐ spending weekly time with them
☐ learning more about them through sports, major, hobbies, arts, experiences with other Christians, beliefs about Christ
☐ looking for ways to serve them
☐ taking risks by inviting them to Bible study, church, chapter meeting, socials, read a Christian book
☐ sharing the gospel with them

I pray for:

1. _____

2. _____

My prayer partner is: _____

phone: _____

My next step(s) to live out 2 PLUS are:

_____

_____

Appendix 2
First Steps to God

The following is an outline of the Christian message that was developed for students and staff in InterVarsity Christian Fellowship. Many have found it a useful summary to keep in mind as they share their faith. You may wish to copy it on the flyleaf of your Bible or photocopy it to carry with you for easy reference.

God
☐ God loves you (John 3:16).
☐ God is holy and just. He punishes all evil and expels it from his presence (Romans 1:18).

People
☐ God, who created everything, made us for himself to find our purpose in fellowship with him (Colossians 1:16).
☐ But we rebelled and turned away from God (Isaiah 53:6). The result is separation from God (Isaiah 59:2). The penalty is eternal death (Romans 6:23).

Christ
☐ God became human in the person of Jesus Christ to restore the broken fellowship (Colossians 1:19-20). Christ lived a perfect life (1 Peter 2:22).
☐ Christ died as a substitute for us by paying the death penalty for our rebellion (Romans 5:8). He arose (1 Corinthians 15:3-4) and is alive today to give us a new life of fellowship with God, now and forever (John 10:10).

Response
☐ I must *repent* for my rebellion (Matthew 4:17).
☐ I must *believe* Christ died to provide forgiveness and a new life of fellowship with God (John 1:12).
☐ I must *receive* Christ as my Savior and Lord with the intent to obey him. I do this in prayer by inviting him into my life (Revelation 3:20).

Cost
☐ There is no cost to you; your salvation comes to you freely (Ephesians 2:8-9).
☐ But it comes at a high cost to God (1 Peter 1:18-19).
☐ Ultimately your response is a life of discipleship (Luke 9:23-24).

Appendix 3
A Code of Ethics for Christian Witness

1. As Christians called by the living God, we seek first of all to honor him and his ethical standards in all of our private and public lives, including our efforts to persuade others to believe the good news about Jesus Christ.

2. As Christian evangelists, we seek to follow the mandate, motives, message and model of our God, who is always pursuing and reclaiming those who are lost in sin and rebellion against him.

3. We believe all people are created in God's image and therefore endowed with the capacity to be in relationship with their Creator and Redeemer. We disavow any efforts to influence people which depersonalize or deprive them of their inherent value as persons.

4. Respecting the value of persons, we believe all people worthy of hearing the gospel of this loving Lord, Jesus Christ. We equally affirm the inalienable right of every person to survey other options and convert to or choose a different belief system.

5. We believe in the gospel of Jesus Christ and affirm the role and goal of the Christian evangelist. However, we do not believe that this justifies any means to fulfill that end. Hence, we disavow the use of any coercive techniques or manipulative appeals that bypass a person's critical faculties, play on psychological weaknesses, undermine relationship with family or religious institutions, or mask the true nature of Christian conversion.

6. While respecting the individual integrity, intellectual honesty and academic freedom of other believers and skeptics, we seek to proclaim Christ openly. We reveal our own identity and purpose, our theological positions and sources of information, and we will not be intentionally misleading. Respect for human integrity means no false advertising, no personal aggrandizement from successfully persuading others to follow Jesus, and no overly emotional appeals which minimize reason and evidence.

7. As Christian evangelists, we seek to embrace people of other religious persuasions in true dialogue. That is, we acknowledge our common humanity as equally sinful, equally needy and equally dependent on the grace of God we proclaim. We seek to listen sensitively in order to understand and thus to divest our witness of any stereotypes or fixed formulas which are barriers to true dialogue.

8. As Christian evangelists, we accept the obligation to admonish one who represents the Christian faith in any manner incompatible with these ethical guidelines.

Revised by Doug Whallon from "A Code of Ethics for the Christian Evangelist," © InterVarsity Christian Fellowship of the United States of America, 1989.

Notes

Chapter 2: First Steps
[1]Actually *The Soul Winner*, by Charles Spurgeon, is a classic, but since Spurgeon wasn't up on late twentieth-century jargon, it didn't compute when I glanced at it.
[2]Paul Little, *The Effective Ambassador* video (2100 Publications, 1976).

Chapter 3: A Father's Rescue
[1]J. I. Packer, *Evangelism and the Sovereignty of God* (Downers Grove, Ill.: InterVarsity Press, 1979), p. 27.

Chapter 4: What I Did on My Spring Break
[1]In chapter ten, I'll offer a platform for apologetics that includes answering both the question and the heartfelt meaning behind the question.
[2]See Lesslie Newbigin, *The Gospel in a Pluralist Society* (Grand Rapids, Mich.: Eerdmans, 1989). Chapter 5 is especially helpful.
[3]James Kennedy is quoted as saying, "While most of the world's Christians have feared the raised fist, we [in America] fear the raised eyebrow."

Chapter 5: Speaking of Jesus
[1]Packer, *Evangelism*, p. 48.
[2]Ibid., p. 49.
[3]You can use the Scripture references in the "First Steps to God" outline to document these statements (see appendix two).
[4]G. K. Chesterton, *Orthodoxy* (New York: John Lane Co., 1909), p. 24.
[5]Some religious professionals are the sad exception. See "The Death of Jesus," *Newsweek*, April 4, 1994, pp. 48-52.
[6]James W. Sire, *Why Should Anyone Believe Anything at All?* (Downers Grove, Ill.: InterVarsity Press, 1994), p. 95.

Chapter 6: Divine Appointments

[1]About six hours if they started at daybreak. Josephus reports that the walk to Jerusalem from Galilee took about three days (*Vita 52.269*).

[2]Walter A. Elwell, ed., *Evangelical Commentary on the Bible* (Grand Rapids, Mich.: Baker, 1989), p. 852.

[3]Bruce Milne, *The Message of John* (Downers Grove, Ill.: InterVarsity Press, 1993), p. 83.

[4]William McDonald, *Believer's Bible Commentary New Testament* (Nashville: Thomas Nelson, 1989), p. 298.

Chapter 7: Jesus Had an Attitude

[1]That was Satan's temptation of Jesus in the desert (Lk 4:3); turning stones to bread represented an evil misuse of power by serving himself rather than others.

Chapter 8: Crossing Barriers

[1]S. S. Bartchy, "Table Fellowship," in *Dictionary of Jesus and the Gospels*, ed. Joel B. Green, Scot McKnight and I. Howard Marshall (Downers Grove, Ill.: InterVarsity Press, 1992), p. 796.

[2]Paul Little, *How to Give Away Your Faith*, second edition (Downers Grove, Ill.: InterVarsity Press, 1988), p. 58.

Chapter 9: The Power of Positive Evangelism

[1]Many of these insights came from a sermon preached by Roy Clements in Eden Chapel, Cambridge, England.

[2]This discussion of Philippians 4:13 is found in Norman Vincent Peale, *The Power of Positive Thinking* (New York: Prentice-Hall, 1952), p. 132.

[3]Quoted in Harold Barrett Robinson and Patricia Cadwallader, *Study Guide for "The Lion, the Witch and the Wardrobe"* (Atlanta, Ga.: Episcopal Radio-TV Foundation, 1979), p. 7.

Chapter 10: The Hooker at the Well

[1]Milne, *The Message of John*, p. 84.

[2]Merrill C. Tenney and Richard Longenecker, "John—Acts," in *Expositor's Bible Commentary*, ed. Frank E. Gaebelein (Grand Rapids, Mich.: Zondervan, 1981), 9:54.

[3]Ibid.

[4]I first heard this view from Pastor John Gichinga of Nairobi Baptist Church.

[5]Craig S. Keener, *The IVP Bible Background Commentary: New Testament* (Downers Grove, Ill.: InterVarsity Press, 1993), p. 273.

[6]This has been a consistent theme of Stott's over the years. Both *Between Two*

Worlds (Grand Rapids, Mich.: Eerdmans, 1982) and *The Contemporary Christian* (Downers Grove, Ill.: InterVarsity Press, 1994) develop these ideas more fully.

[7]This is the first part of what Stott calls "double listening": listening to the world and listening to the Word.

Chapter 11: Questions
[1]Gene Breitenbach in *The IVY Jungle Report* 2 (Spring 1994): 1.

[2]See William Dyrness, *Christian Apologetics in a World Community* (Downers Grove, Ill.: InterVarsity Press, 1982), especially pp. 19-22.

[3]Peter Kreeft and Ronald K. Tacelli, *Handbook of Christian Apologetics* (Downers Grove, Ill.: InterVarsity Press, 1994), p. 21.

[4]Dyrness, *Christian Apologetics*, p. 19.

[5]Ibid., p. 24.

Chapter 12: Answers
[1]Kreeft and Tacelli, *Handbook of Christian Apologetics*, p. 122. There are over twenty proofs for theism (see chapter 3).

[2]Given the right context, I might add, "And any religious system too."

Chapter 13: Telling Our Story
[1]Josephus *Antiquities* 4.8.15, section 219.

[2]John White, *Daring to Draw Near* (Downers Grove, Ill.: InterVarsity Press, 1977), p. 8.

Chapter 14: The Big Picture
[1]Walter M. Dunnett, "Nero," in *Wycliffe Bible Encyclopedia*, ed. Charles F. Pfeiffer, Howard F. Vos and John Rea (Chicago: Moody Press, 1975), 2:1199.

[2]Murphy-O'Connor estimates the size of the church to be about fifty people, based on excavations and the listing of the fourteen male members in 1 and 2 Corinthians. S. J. Hafemann, "Corinthians, Letters to the," in *Dictionary of Paul and His Letters*, ed. Gerald F. Hawthorne, Ralph P. Martin and Daniel G. Reid (Downers Grove, Ill.: InterVarsity Press, 1993), p. 173.

[3]Ibid.

[4]Ibid.

[5]Four sections of Paul's writing frame reconciliation as Paul's theological center: Romans 5:8-11; 2 Corinthians 5:18-21; Ephesians 2:14-17; Colossians 1:20-22.

[6]Yitzhak Rabin, "Enough of Blood and Tears," *Vital Speeches of the Day*, October 1, 1993, pp. 740-41.

[7]Yitzhak Rabin, "Peace at Last?" *Newsweek*, September 13, 1993, p. 21.

[8]S. E. Porter, "Peace, Reconciliation," in *Dictionary of Paul and His Letters,* p 697.

[9]John Stott notes that the image of the cross is a meeting of horizontal and vertical (*The Cross of Christ* [Downers Grove, Ill.: InterVarsity Press, 1986], p. 21).

[10]I'm not the only one. See Mark A. Noll, *A History of Christianity in the United States and Canada* (Grand Rapids, Mich.: Eerdmans, 1992), pp. 199, 217.

Chapter 15: Ambassadorship
[1]See Charles Colson, *Kingdoms in Conflict* (Grand Rapids, Mich.: Zondervan, 1987).

Chapter 16: Immigration
[1]The same is true of the other two times this word is used in the New Testament. See Packer, *Evangelism,* p. 49.

[2]Ibid., p. 50.

[3]I know I've come close to a theological term here—sorry. For fans of H. Richard Niebuhr, I would refer you to Stanley Hauerwas and William H. Willimon, *Resident Aliens* (Nashville: Abingdon Press, 1989), p. 43. They make a persuasive argument that Niebuhr's idea of Christ and culture is one of the great twentieth-century heresies. They say that Christianity does not define itself by social strategy; it *is* social strategy.

Chapter 17: Establishing Residency
[1]P. Beasley-Murray, "Pastor, Paul as," in *Dictionary of Paul and His Letters,* p. 654.

[2]See, for example, 1 Corinthians 3:1-3; Galatians 4:19; 1 Thessalonians 2:7-8 for the image of motherhood and 1 Corinthians 4:15; 1 Thessalonians 2:11; Philemon 10 for the image of fatherhood.

[3]Beasley-Murray, "Pastor, Paul as," p. 657.

[4]See 1 Corinthians 4:14-16; 11:1; Galatians 4:12; Philippians 3:17; 1 Thessalonians 1:6.

[5]The International Bible Society sells all kinds of Bibles at affordable prices. Write the International Bible Society, P.O. Box 62970, Colorado Springs, CO 80962-2970 for a catalog. They even have a university edition geared for college seekers.

[6]Beasley-Murray, "Pastor, Paul as," p. 658.

[7]Talk to your pastor, or call the American Association of Christian Counselors (AACC) at (800) 5-COUNSEL, or the Christian Association of Psychological Studies (CAPS) at (210) 629-CAPS for referral lists of Christian counselors in your area.

Speaking of Jesus, a video series featuring Mack Stiles and the material in this book, is also available for purchase from InterVarsity Press. To rent the series, write InterVarsity Video at P.O. Box 7895, Madison, WI 53707-7895, or phone (800) 828-2100.